D0854549

Students and External F

DATE DUE FOR RETURN | DATE OF ISSUE

12 MAR

UNIVERSITY OF NOTTINGHAM

WITHDRAWN FROM THE LIBRARY

TELEPEN

6 00 019068 2

THE HOME UNIVERSITY LIBRARY OF MODERN KNOWLEDGE

1

PARLIAMENT

EDITORS OF
The Home University Library of Modern Knowledge

GILBERT MURRAY, O.M., D.C.L., F.B.A.

G. N. CLARK, LL.D., F.B.A.

G. R. DE BEER, D.SC., F.R.S.

United States

JOHN FULTON, M.D., PH.D.

HOWARD MUMFORD JONES, LITT.D.

WILLIAM L. LANGER, PH.D.

Parliament

Its History, Constitution, and Practice

SIR COURTENAY ILBERT

REVISED BY SIR CECIL CARR

Third Edition

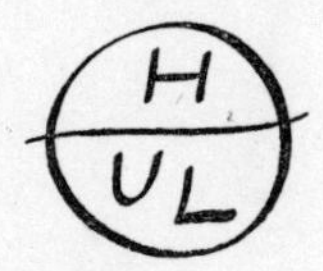

Geoffrey Cumberlege

OXFORD UNIVERSITY PRESS

LONDON NEW YORK TORONTO

1948

First published in 1911 *and reprinted in* 1912, 1917, 1918, *and* 1919. Second edition 1920, *reprinted in* 1922, 1924, 1925, 1926, 1927, 1929, 1932, 1936, *and* 1939. Third edition (*revised by* Sir Cecil Carr *and entirely reset*) 1948.

PRINTED IN GREAT BRITAIN

PREFACE TO THIRD EDITION

This little book first appeared in 1911. In a preface to his second edition, written in the summer of 1919, the author explained that his pages were designed 'to be an introduction to the history, constitution and practice of parliament as it was constituted and worked before the war'. He had revised them in the light of the considerable changes due to such events as the Representation of the People Act 1918. 'But there are parts of the book', he wrote, 'which relate to institutions now in a state of flux and which it was therefore necessary to leave as they stood.' He mentioned in particular the suspension of the party system in 1915 and of the cabinet system at the end of 1916. 'It is as yet impossible to say', he added, 'when or in what form they will reappear.' In a subsequent reprint a postscript to this preface was able to record that the cabinet system had been formally restored in October 1919, and the party system in October 1922.

Events and vicissitudes no less significant set similar problems for an editor in 1947. Enactments like the Irish constitutional changes and the Statute of Westminster can be stated definitely enough. But another World War, wherein the very meeting-place of the Commons House of Parliament has been completely destroyed, has accustomed us to so prolonged a period of emergency and so convenient, swift, and elastic a technique of departmental law-making that it is difficult to predict when, or within what limits, the traditional methods of direct legislation, the result of public and reasonably deliberate discussion in parliament, will return. In the present revision the additions attempt to describe the relations between the two Houses since the passing of the Parliament Act, the progressive delegation of legislative power, and the search for fresh expedients directed towards extracting the maximum output from a session. The chapter which formerly covered Finance and Administration has now been split into two. In the final chapter where the author contrasted the constitutions of other nations with that of Britain, the references to legislatures and governments in the countries on the continent of Europe have been omitted. In Ilbert's second edition they were retained, though with a word of caution. In the present fluidity and uncertainty it seems premature to include them. A glossary of terms in parliamentary use has been appended.

Whatever the anxieties of modification, the book remains in substance as it was first written. Its pages continue to attest its author's mastery of his subject. No apology is needed if a few sentences are added here in honour of his memory. Courtenay Peregrine Ilbert had a brilliant academic career. Going up to Oxford from Marlborough as a scholar of Balliol, he won the Hertford, Ireland, and Craven scholarships and became a fellow of his college. Oxford gave him the friendship of Jowett (whose literary executor he became) and of Bryce; among his pupils was H. H. Asquith. Ilbert was called to the bar in 1869. That year saw the establishment of the office of the Parliamentary Counsel to the Treasury with Sir Henry Thring (afterwards Lord Thring) as its first holder. Thring had been acting as a parliamentary draftsman since 1850, at first unofficially, afterwards as

Home Office Counsel. Ilbert, though by no means idle at the bar, found time to work at drafting statutes under Thring. With his friend Mackenzie Chalmers he had a hand in framing the Bills which became the Statute Law Revision Act of 1881, and the Civil Procedure Act of 1883, a sequel to the important changes made by the Judicature Acts in the work of the courts. Then followed a few years in India as Law Member of the Governor-General's Council, a post which had earlier attracted men of the calibre of Macaulay, Maine, and James Fitzjames Stephen. From India Ilbert eventually returned to London to be assistant Parliamentary Counsel under Sir Henry Jenkyns, who by this time had succeeded Thring. He himself succeeded Jenkyns in 1899. 'The particular qualities of Ilbert's mind, its penetration, its precision, its good sense in judging between two views, operated', Lord Simon has recently said, 'in the most surprising degree to improve the output, in form as well as in substance, of our legislation.' In 1902 he was appointed Clerk of the House of Commons. If he did not bring to his new position the deep knowledge of the unwritten law and practice of parliament which comes by long experience to veteran members and officials of the House, he had exceptional equipment as a constitutional lawyer and as an expert in the technical processes of law-making. His volume on *Legislative Methods and Forms* became a classic. He lectured in the United States with great acceptance on the matters which he had made his own. His advice was sought by correspondents in many countries. He was the chief founder of the Society of Comparative Legislation. He was an energetic chairman of the Statute Law Committee, 'whose useful operations [wrote his friend Sir Frederick Pollock] are a mystery to the lay public, not too well understood by the majority of lawyers, and unheeded by party politicians for whom showy new legislation, often spoilt by haste and improvident compromise, is more attractive than the weeding out and consolidation of the old.'

This interest in the improvement of the statute-book Ilbert retained till his death in 1924. It was, he used to say, a little garden which he wished to cultivate until the end.

Nearly fifty years ago he wrote that the function of parliament was—as it had been for the past six centuries —to remove discontent and to avert revolution by making laws which adapted the political, administrative, and economical arrangements of the country to the requirements of the times. Its legislation, he added, had grown ever more complicated; most of it was administrative in character, not 'lawyers' law'. To the exacting task of framing such legislation Ilbert himself devoted, like others before and after him, an exceptional combination of scholarship and practical wisdom. It happened to him, as to many eminent public servants, that the major part of his work was, by its very nature, produced in forms which could only be anonymous. His name should be remembered.

CECIL CARR

September 1947

CONTENTS

CHAP.		PAGE
	Preface to Third Edition	v
I.	Origin and Development	1
II.	Constitution of the House of Commons	21
III.	The Making of Laws	52
IV.	Finance	76
V.	Administration	96
VI.	Sittings and Procedure	104
VII.	Organization of the House	124
VIII.	The Member and his Constituents	139
IX.	Records, the Press, and the Public	153
X.	The House of Lords	169
XI.	Comparative	193
	Glossary	205
	Bibliography	216
	Index	223

CHAPTER I

ORIGIN AND DEVELOPMENT

THE WORD 'parliament' originally meant a talk. In its Latin form it is applied by monastic statutes of the thirteenth century to the talk held by monks in their cloisters after dinner, talk which the statutes condemn as unedifying. A little later the term was used to describe solemn conferences such as that held in 1245 between Louis IX of France and Pope Innocent IV. When our Henry III summoned a council or conference of great men to discuss grievances he was said by a contemporary chronicler to hold a parliament. The word struck root in England, and was soon applied regularly to the national assemblies which were summoned from time to time by Henry's great successor, Edward I, and which took something like definite shape in what was afterwards called the 'Model Parliament' of 1295. The word, as we have seen, signified at first the talk itself, the conference held, not the persons holding it. By degrees it was transferred to the body of persons assembled for conference, just as the word 'conference' itself has a double meaning. When Edward I was holding his parliaments, institutions of the same kind were growing up in France. But the body which in France bore the same name as the English parliament had a different history and a different fate. The French 'parlement' became a judicial institution, though it claimed to have a share in the making of laws.

The history of the English parliament may be roughly

divided into four great periods: the period of the medieval parliaments, of which the parliament of 1295 became the model and type; the period of the Tudors and Stuarts, having for its central portion the time of conflict between king and parliament, between prerogative and privilege; the period between the Revolution of 1688 and the Reform Act of 1832; and the modern period which began in 1832.

Let us try and trace, in broad outline, the elements out of which the parliament of 1295 grew up, and the main stages through which its development passed.

It had always been regarded in England as a principle that in grave and important matters, such as the making of laws, the king ought not to act without counsel and consent. The counsel and consent which the Saxon kings sought was that of their wise men, and the 'witenagemot' of English constitutional history was a meeting of these wise men. It seems, says Maitland, to have been a very unstable and indefinite body. It was an assembly of the great folk. When there was a strong king, it was much in his power to say how the assembly should be constituted and whom he would summon. When the king was weak, the assembly was apt to be anarchical. The Saxon witenagemot was not numerous. Small men, especially if they lived at a distance, could not come. Great men often would not come. The institution was not much of a safeguard against oppression. Still it was an important fact that, on the eve of the Norman conquest, no English king had taken on himself to legislate or tax without the counsel and consent of a national assembly, an assembly of the wise, that is, of the great.

The Norman conquest made a great break in English

institutions, but not so great as was at one time supposed. In the first place William the Conqueror had to build with English materials and on English foundations. In the next place English institutions had, during the reign of Edward the Confessor, been rapidly approximating to the continental type. What William did was to emphasize, rather than to introduce, certain principles of what was afterwards vaguely described as the 'feudal system', and to adapt them to his own purposes. He insisted on the principle that all land in the country was ultimately held of the king. There were to be no full owners of land under him, only holders or tenants. He insisted on the principle that every landholder in the country owed direct allegiance to the king. The landholder might hold his land under, and owe allegiance to, another lord, but his oath of allegiance to that lord was qualified by his allegiance to the king. And, in portioning out the English soil among the motley band of adventurers who had followed him and whom he had to reward for their share in his raid, he tried to break the strength of the greater men by scattering their estates over different parts of England, and by mixing up with them smaller men who held their land, not under any intermediate lord, but directly under the king. He did not wholly succeed, as he and those after him found to their cost. But the existence, by the side of the greater lords, of a number of comparatively small landholders, who also held their land directly from the king, had an important bearing on the development of parliament. The Norman kings were despots, untrammelled by any constitutional restrictions, and controlled only by the resistance of powerful and turbulent subjects. But there were the traditions of better things past; there were the charters, often broken but always there, by the help of which kings with doubtful titles obtained succession, and in which they promised to observe those traditions; and there was a feeling that, apart from these promises, it was prudent and politic to obtain an expression of counsel and consent, if it could be obtained.

'Thrice a year [says the Saxon chronicle of the Conqueror] King William wore his crown every year he was in England; at Easter he wore it at Winchester, at Pentecost at Westminster, and at Christmas at Gloucester; and at these times all the men of England were with him, archbishops, bishops and abbots, earls, thegns and knights.'

'All the men of England'—what did this mean? To the Saxon chronicler it probably meant the men who counted, the wise and great, the men who might have been expected to attend a witenagemot. But William's court was a feudal court, and from the Norman point of view perhaps it was an assembly of the king's tenants in chief. These, however, were numerous, and many of them were small men, so that probably only a select few were summoned. Courts or great councils of the same kind were held under the later Norman kings, but we know little about their composition or functions. All that can be said with safety is that the few legislative acts of this period were done with the counsel and consent of the great men.

What we find is the transformation of the body whose counsel and consent is required from a merely feudal body, a body of great vassals or tenants in chief, to a body more representative of the nation at large.

Henry II did something when he imposed a tax on movables, the Saladin tithe of 1188, and had it assessed by a jury of neighbours, a jury in some sense representative of the taxpayer and of the parish in which he lived. This brought into connexion the ideas of taxation and representation.

The Great Charter of 1215 declared that exceptional feudal aids were not to be levied without the common counsel of the realm. But this counsel was to be given by an assembly consisting of prelates and great lords summoned singly, and of tenants in chief summoned collectively through the sheriffs. So it was still a feudal assembly.

A further step was taken when, in 1254, at a time when Henry III was in great need of money, each sheriff was required to send two knights from his county to consider what aid they would give the king in his great necessity. For these knights represented, not the tenants in chief, but all the free men of their county. They were representatives of counties.

Eleven years later, in 1265, Simon de Montfort summoned to his famous parliament representatives not merely of counties but also of cities and boroughs.

Edward I held several great assemblies, which were usually called parliaments. They made some great laws, but some of these laws were made without the assent of representatives of the commons.

The Model Parliament, which settled the general type for all future times, was held in 1295. To this parliament King Edward summoned separately the two archbishops, all the bishops, the greater abbots, seven earls, and forty-one barons. The archbishops and bishops were directed to bring the heads of their cathedral chapters, their archdeacons, one proctor for the clergy of each cathedral, and two proctors for the clergy of each diocese. Every sheriff was directed to cause two knights of each shire, two citizens of each city, and two burgesses of each borough, to be elected.

Two points should be specially noticed about the constitution of this parliament.

In the first place it was not a feudal court, nor a meeting of the king's tenants, but a national assembly. Edward had suffered much in his father's time from the great barons who had made him prisoner at the battle of Lewes; he wished to draw counsel and help from other quarters. His parliament was intended to represent the three great estates or classes into which medieval society might be roughly divided, the clergy, the barons, and the commons—those who pray, those who fight, and those who work, as Maitland put it. The same idea underlay the States General which were coming into existence about the same time in France, and which met at intervals, during many centuries. After an interval of 175 years the three estates of France were for the last time summoned to meet as separate bodies in 1789, but were at once merged in the national assembly which began the French Revolution.

The idea of the three estates was never realized in England. The clause by which archbishops and bishops were directed to bring with them representatives of their clergy, a clause still remaining in the writ by which they are summoned at the present day, was persistently ignored. The clergy as a body preferred to stand aloof, to meet in their own clerical assemblies or convocations, and to settle there what contribution they would make to the king's needs. The archbishops, bishops, and greater abbots attended, as they had attended the great councils of previous kings. But then they were not merely clerics, they were great feudal lords and great holders of land.

The knights of the shires were drawn from the same class as the greater barons. The word 'baron' originally meant simply 'man', and for some time there was much uncertainty as to who should be treated as a man so great as to be entitled to a separate summons, and who should be left to be represented, like other freemen of the lesser sort, by the knights of the shires. The title of baron came eventually to be confined to the greater men who were summoned separately. The knights who represented the shires, when they came to Westminster, mingled themselves with the representatives of the cities and boroughs. In the time of Edward III there was a risk of the merchants being consulted as a separate class for the purpose of taxation, but this risk was avoided. If things had fallen out somewhat differently the English parliament might have sat as three separate houses, as in France, or might have been grouped in a single house, as in Scotland, or might have formed four houses, as in Sweden. But the inferior clergy abstained from attendance; the greater clergy, the spiritual lords, sat with the lay or temporal lords; and the knights of the shires threw in their lot with the citizens and burgesses. Thus parliament became an assembly, not of three estates, but of two houses, the house consisting of the lords spiritual and temporal, and the house representing the commons, the House of Lords and the House of Commons.

The other point to be noticed is that parliament was an expansion, for temporary purposes, of the king's continuous council. The Norman and Plantagenet kings, like other kings, needed continuous assistance—for domestic and ceremonial purposes, and for the business of government, such as the administration of justice and the collection and expenditure of revenue. The courts or councils composed of the men on whom the king most relied for this assistance bore various names, varied in number, and exercised varying functions. As the work of government increased and specialized, these nebulous bodies split up into more coherent parts, with more definite functions, and out of them grew the king's courts of justice and the great departments of the central government. When the king held his great assemblies, it was necessary that he should have about him the men on whom he was accustomed to place special reliance for advice and assistance. Accordingly there were summoned by name to the parliament of 1295 men who were not earls or barons, but were members of the king's council, and in particular the king's judges. And to this day the judges of the Supreme Court are summoned to parliament, and some of them take their seats in the House of Lords when the king opens parliament.

The fact that the medieval parliament was an expansion of the king's council explains the nature of the business which it had to transact. The immediate cause of summoning a parliament was usually want of money. The king had incurred, or was about to incur, expenses which he could not meet out of his ordinary resources such as the revenues of his domain and the usual feudal dues. He summoned a parliament and, through his chancellor or some other minister, explained what he wanted and why he wanted it. The king's speech might touch on other great matters about which he might need advice or approval, but money was the gist. On the other hand the king's subjects had grievances for which they desired redress. The grievances would be of different kinds, breach of old customs, failure to observe charters or laws, oppression by the king's officers or by great men, maladministration of justice, difficulties in the way of settling private disputes, and so forth. For the redress of these grievances petitions were presented, petitions which in their multifarious character were not unlike the statements of grievances presented to the national assembly on the eve of the French Revolution. The petitions were to the king in parliament or to the king in his council, and parliament was the petitioning body, the body by or through whom the petitions were presented. The remedies required would be classified in modern language as judicial, legislative, or administrative. But in the thirteenth century these distinctions had not been clearly drawn. A statute made by Edward I in his parliament of 1292, known as the Statute of Waste, based on a petition presented to him in that parliament, supplies a good illustration of the way in which judicial, legislative, and administrative remedies might be combined. The statute begins with a long story showing how Gawin Butler brought a complaint before the king's justices about waste done to his land, but died before obtaining judgement; how his brother and heir, William, who was under age and a ward of the king, sought to continue the proceedings; and how the justices differed in opinion as to whether he was entitled to do so. Thereupon the king, in his full parliament, by his common council or by general consent (for the Latin phrase wavers between the two meanings of 'council' and 'counsel') ordains that all heirs may have an action by writ of waste for waste done in the time of their ancestors, and the king himself commands his justices to give judgement accordingly. Here the king acts partly in his legislative capacity, laying down a general rule, partly in his judicial capacity, as having power to review and control the proceedings of his justices, and partly in an administrative capacity as guardian of an infant heir.

At the beginning of each parliament the king, or his great council on his behalf, appointed persons to receive and to try these petitions, that is to say to sort them out, to consider what remedy, if any, each petition required, and to devise an appropriate form of remedy. The triers or auditors of petitions were really committees of the king's council. Until near the close of the nineteenth century receivers and triers of petitions from England, Scotland, and Gascony respectively (for Edward I ruled in Gascony as well as England) were appointed at the beginning of each parliament by an entry in the Lords Journals. But their functions had ceased for many centuries.

The sittings of an early Plantagenet parliament did not extend over many days. Travelling was difficult, dangerous, and costly; members could not afford to stay long away from their homes. The main object of the meeting was usually to strike a bargain between the king and his subjects. The king wanted a grant of money, and it was made a condition of the grant that certain grievances, about which petitions had been presented, should be redressed. When an agreement had been arrived at as to how much money should be granted and on what terms, the commoners and most of the lords went their ways, leaving the king's advisers, the members of his council, to devise and work out, by means of legislation or otherwise, such remedies as might be considered appropriate and advisable.

It is to the Plantagenet period that we owe the most

picturesque of our parliamentary ceremonials, those which attend the opening of parliament and the signification of the royal assent to Acts. Perhaps we might think of the Plantagenet parliament as something like an oriental durbar held by an Amir of Afghanistan, with the king sitting on his throne, attended by his courtiers and great chiefs, hearing the complaints of his subjects and determining whether and how they should be met.

Of the changes in the composition of parliament which took place during this period something will be said later; but a few words must be said here about the changes in its powers and functions, especially with respect to the two main branches of its business, namely taxation and legislation.

Before the end of the fourteenth century parliament had established two principles of taxation. In the first place they had taken away the power of the king to impose direct taxes without their consent, and had restricted his power to impose indirect taxes without their consent to such taxes as might be justified under the customs recognized by the Great Charter. In the second place parliament had acquired the right to impose taxes, direct and indirect, of all kinds. In imposing these taxes they did not care to go beyond the immediate needs of the case. Hence the necessity for frequent parliaments.

According to the theory of the three estates, each estate would tax itself separately, and this theory was at first observed. The clergy granted their subsidies, not in parliament, but in convocation, and they continued to do so, in theory at least, until after the Restoration of 1660. But long before this time they had agreed to grant or submit to taxes corresponding to those imposed on the laity. At a much earlier date, before the end of the fourteenth century, the lords and commons, instead of making separate grants, agreed to join in a common grant. And, as the bulk of the burden fell upon the commons, they adopted a formula which placed the commons in the foreground. The grant was made by the commons, with the consent of the lords spiritual and temporal. This formula appeared in 1395, and became the rule. In 1407, eight years after Henry IV came to the throne, he assented to the important principle that money grants were to be initiated by the House of Commons, were not to be reported to the king until both houses were agreed, and were to be reported by the Speaker of the Commons House. This rule is strictly observed at the present day. When a money Bill, such as the Finance Bill for the year or the Appropriation Bill, has been passed by the House of Commons and agreed to by the House of Lords it is, unlike all other Bills, returned to the House of Commons. On the day for signifying the royal assent the Clerk of the House of Commons takes it up to the bar of the House of Lords, then hands it to the Speaker, who delivers it with his own hand to the officer charged with signifying the king's assent, the Clerk of Parliaments.

Ever since the reign of Henry VII the enacting formula of Acts of Parliament has run thus—

> 'Be it enacted by the King's [or Queen's] most Excellent Majesty, by and with the advice and consent of the Lords Spiritual and Temporal, and Commons, in this present Parliament assembled, and by the authority of the same, as follows.'

This formula grew into shape in what has been called above the medieval period of parliament. At the beginning of this period the king made laws with the requisite advice and consent. One important early Act was expressed to be made at the instance of the great men. Later the concurrence of the whole parliament, including the commons, became essential. But the commons usually appear at first in a subordinate position. Throughout the fourteenth century the kind of form most usually adopted is that a statute is made with the assent of the earls, prelates, and barons and at the request of the knights of the shires and commons in parliament assembled. The commons appear as petitioners for laws rather than as legislators. And this is in fact what they were. They presented their petitions, which might ask for amendment or clearer declaration of the law. It was for the king, with the aid of those more intimately in his counsels, to determine whether legislation was required and if so what form it should assume. Throughout the fourteenth century there was much risk that, even if the making of a law were granted, the law, when made, would not correspond to the petition on which it was based. The statute was not drawn up until after the parliament was dissolved; its form was settled by the king's council, and there were many complaints about the variance between petitions and statutes. At last in 1414, soon after the accession of Henry V, the king conceded the point for which the commons had repeatedly pressed. The commons prayed 'that there never be no law made and engrossed as statute and law neither by additions nor discriminations by no manner of term or terms which should change the sentence and the intent asked'. And the king in reply granted that from henceforth 'nothing be enacted to the petition of the commons contrary to their asking, whereby they should be bound without their assent'. This concession led to an important change in the method of framing statutes. It became the practice to send up to the king, not a petition, but a Bill drawn in the form of a statute, so that the king was left no alternative beyond assent or dissent. Legislation by Bill took the place of legislation on petition. This practice became settled about the end of the reign of Henry VI.

The changes in practice were reflected by changes in the legislative formula. Statutes were expressed to be made by the advice and consent of the lords and the commons, thus putting the two houses on an equal footing. And before the middle of the fifteenth century a significant addition was made to the formula. Statutes were expressed to be made, not only with the advice and consent of the lords and commons in parliament, but 'by the authority of the same'. This was an admission that the statute derived its authority from the whole parliament. The two houses had become not merely an advising, consenting, or petitioning body, but a legislative authority.

The power to refuse assent to legislation still remained, and it was often exercised until a much later date. It was signified in a courteous form—'The king will consider.'

The political power of parliament grew rapidly in the fourteenth and fifteenth centuries. In 1327 a parliament which had been summoned in the name of Edward II resolved, in summary fashion, on his deposition and forced him to resign. But the proceedings on the deposition of Richard II were more formal. Richard was forced to summon a parliament, and then to execute a deed of resignation. The parliament assembled in Westminster Hall, which Richard had rebuilt, and which stood then much as it stands now. Parliament accepted his resignation and went on, by further resolutions, to declare that he was deposed and to resolve that Henry of Lancaster should be king in his place. A parliament which could thus make and unmake kings was a formidable body. The Lancastrian kings, it has been said, were kings by Act of Parliament; they meant to rule and did rule by means of parliament. In the quarrels of the seventeenth century between king and commons men looked back to the Lancastrian period as the golden age of parliament, and precedents from that period were freely quoted for parliamentary use. But in the fifteenth century the times were not ripe for parliamentary government. The powers of parliament fell into the hands of turbulent nobles. Henry V was a famous and capable warrior. But Henry VI began his reign as an infant, and ended it as an idiot; he was ruled by unscrupulous uncles and a termagant queen; and the bloody faction fights known as the Wars of the Roses brought the Plantagenet dynasty to a close, weeded out the older nobility, and cleared the way for a new form of monarchy.

The age of the Tudors, at least during the reigns of Henry VIII and Elizabeth, is a period of strong monarchs governing through the strength of parliament. Henry VIII accepted Henry IV's principle that the king should rule through parliament, but worked that principle in an entirely different way. He made parliament the engine of his will. He persuaded or frightened it into doing anything he pleased. Under his guidance parliament defied and crushed all other powers, spiritual and temporal, and did things which no king or parliament had ever attempted to do, things unheard of and terrible. Elizabeth scolded her parliaments for meddling with matters with which, in her opinion, they had no concern; more than once she soundly rated the Speaker of her commons. But she never carried her quarrels too far and was always able to end her disputes by some clever compromise. The result was that her parliaments usually acquiesced in and gave effect to her wishes. Before Henry VIII the life of parliament was usually comprised within a single session, and the sessions were short. Parliaments now grew longer. Henry VIII's Reformation parliament lasted for seven years. One of Elizabeth's parliaments lasted for eleven years, though, it is true, it held only three sessions. Parliament was no longer a meeting dissolved as soon as some specific business was finished. It tended to become a permanent power in the State, and a power with formidable attributes. A monarch who swayed and did not fear parliament could afford to recognize its sovereignty, for it was his own. And never were the authority and sovereignty of parliament more emphatically asserted than in Tudor times. Sir Thomas Smith, secretary to Queen Elizabeth, declares in a book which was published in 1589, and which he called *The Commonwealth of England and the manner of government thereof*, that 'the most high and absolute power of the realm of England consisteth in the parliament'. Such doctrines could be preached with safety while Tudor kingcraft remained; when it departed they shook and upset the throne.

It was in Tudor times that both houses began to keep their journals and that the House of Commons acquired a permanent home of their own. But these are matters of which more will be said hereafter. Owing to the existence of the journals we now begin to know much more about the proceedings of parliament than in previous times. Under the Plantagenets some of the characteristic features of parliamentary procedure, such as the three readings of Bills, had been settled, but had not been recorded. In the journals the dates of each reading are given. The entries are at first scanty, but are soon amplified. Rulings and practices are noted, precedents are searched for and observed. The records of the Elizabethan journals are expanded by Sir Symonds d'Ewes from other sources. Sir Thomas Smith, in the book already mentioned, and Hooker, in the book which he wrote for the guidance of the parliament at Dublin, have given us descriptions which enable us to understand how business was conducted in the English parliament under the great queen. The general outlines of parliamentary procedure were settled, and much of the common law of parliament, the law which is not to be found in Standing Orders, may be traced back to Elizabethan times.

James I came to the throne by inheritance. He talked much and foolishly about his divine right to rule, and soon came into collision with his parliaments. Parliament claimed and obtained some important rights, such as the right to adjourn without the king's leave, and the right to determine disputes about the validity of elections. Other questions, such as the right to levy taxes, remained to be fought out under his successor. The king and parliament were hostile bodies, and parliament was jealous of the king's interference with, or even knowledge of, its proceedings.

The main lines of parliamentary procedure were settled during the seventeenth century. The committee system grew up under Elizabeth and her successor. Small committees were appointed to consider the details of Bills and other matters, and sat either at Westminster or sometimes at the Temple or elsewhere. For weightier matters larger committees were appointed. These tended to include all members who were willing to come, for the difficulty was to obtain a quorum. Hence the system of grand committees, and of committees of the whole House, which will be described in a later chapter. Before the end of the seventeenth century parliamentary procedure began to follow the lines which it retained until after the Reform Act of 1832. The first edition of Sir Erskine May's book on parliamentary procedure was published in 1844, and 'the parliamentary procedure of 1844', says Sir R. Palgrave in his preface to the tenth edition, 'was essentially the procedure on which the House of Commons conducted its business during the Long Parliament'.

The constitutional quarrel of the seventeenth century, which culminated in the great civil war, was at first whether government should be by the king or by the king in parliament, afterwards whether the king should govern or whether parliament should govern. Strafford, the strong minister of a weak king, tried to govern without parliament, and failed. The Long Parliament tried to govern without a king, and failed. During the revolutionary period the House of Commons set up executive committees, foreshadowing the famous executive committees of the French Revolution; but government by committees was not a success. The great rule of Cromwell was a series of failures to reconcile the authority of the 'single person' with the authority of parliament. The monarchical régime which was revived under Charles II broke down under James II. It was left for the 'glorious revolution' of 1688, and for the Hanoverian dynasty, to develop the ingenious system of adjustments and compromises which is now known, sometimes as Cabinet government, sometimes as parliamentary government. Of the growth and working of this system more will be said hereafter.

The two last of the parliamentary periods referred to above must be passed over very lightly. The eighteenth century was a great age of parliamentary oratory, but it was not an age of great legislation. The territorial magnates who, or whose nominees, as knights of the shires or members for pocket boroughs, constituted the House of Commons, contented themselves in the main with formulating as Acts of Parliament rules for the guidance of landowners as justices of the peace. Parliamentary procedure tended to stiffen and become more formal. Important constitutional changes were silently going on, but they were not, as a rule, marked by legislation. One of the few exceptions was the Septennial Act of 1715, which extended from three years, the limit fixed by an Act of 1694, to seven years, the maximum duration of a parliament, a period eventually reduced to five years by the Parliament Act, 1911. In the eighteenth century power rested first with the families of the great Whig magnates who had brought about the Revolution of 1688, then for a time with the king and his 'friends', and finally with the parliamentary genius whom George III was fortunate enough to obtain as chief adviser, the younger Pitt.

The earthquake of the French Revolution, which shook all Europe, and changed its surface, did not extend across the English Channel. It produced effects here, but its immediate effects were those of resistance and reaction, and its results were to prolong the period of the old régime for more than thirty years after the close of the eighteenth century.

Leipzig and Waterloo stopped the course of the Revolution in Europe. But, after a trial of fifteen years, the revived French monarchy of the Restoration died in the Paris barricades of 1830. Two years later the Act o 1832 reformed the constitution of the House of Commons, and brought fresh powers into play. After the lapse of another two years the fire of 16 October 1834 destroyed the ancient home of parliament. Of the buildings which had sheltered parliaments for so many centuries nothing remained above ground except the great hall which William Rufus built and Richard II rebuilt, and some parts of the cloisters which were added to St. Stephen's Chapel shortly before the dissolution of its chapter. The new parliament had to build a new home, the home which, despite the violence of enemy action in the wars of 1914 and 1939, still remains within the Palace of Westminster.

CHAPTER II

CONSTITUTION OF THE HOUSE OF COMMONS

It is from no disrespect for the House of Lords that the description of that House is reserved for a later chapter, but because the principal share of parliamentary business is transacted in the House of Commons; because the position of the older house is, under our constitution, subordinate; and because the position and functions of the House of Lords cannot be understood until the functions of the House of Commons have been explained.

A double thread of meaning runs through the word 'commons'. Technically, the house of commons, at the time of its institution, was the community or body representing the communities of the counties and of the boroughs.

'The commons [says Stubbs] are the communities, the organized bodies of freemen of the shires and towns, and the estate of the commons is the general body into which, for the purposes of parliament, these communities are combined.'

But the word has another shade of meaning, reflected in the modern use of the word 'commoner'. The commons are those who are not included in either of the special classes of clergy and barons. 'The persons who enjoy no special privilege,' says Maitland, 'who have no peculiar status of barons or clerks, are common men.' In this sense they correspond to the third estate of France, which, on the eve of the French Revolution, according to Sieyès, was nothing, wished to be something, and ought to be everything.

The technical meaning of the word is, for historical purposes, of great importance. Before the time of parliaments both the counties and the boroughs had been recognized as communities for judicial, fiscal, and administrative purposes, and the counties acted as such in their county courts which were local assemblies very different from the judicial tribunals of that name to-day. The boroughs were winning for themselves, through charters, communal rights resembling and often suggested by those of the French communes. It was but a step forward to utilize existing ideas and institutions for the purpose of national and parliamentary representation.

The history of the county franchise is comparatively simple. The sheriffs were directed by their writs to cause an election to be held of two knights for each shire; election was to be made in and by the county court, and the electors were those who were entitled to attend and take part in the proceedings of that court. No further definition of the machinery of election was attempted, or was, at first, necessary. The sheriff would conduct the proceedings in the customary fashion, and would have a good deal to say as to who should take part in them. It was not until the reign of Henry VI that any statutory restriction was placed on the class of electors. The Act of 1430, which was passed to prevent riotous and disorderly elections, directed that the electors were to be people dwelling in the county, whereof everyone was to have free land or tenement to the value of forty shillings a year at least (a high value for that period) above all charges. This Act continued to regulate the county franchise for more than four centuries, until the Reform

Act of 1832. But the definition of the qualifying freehold gave much employment to lawyers and parliamentary committees, and its meaning was so interpreted as to facilitate the manufacture of qualifications and the creation of 'faggot voters', a single tenement being subdivided among several nominal owners as one might separate the sticks in a bundle. Leaseholders and copyholders had no votes.

The number of parliamentary counties did not vary much before 1832. At first there were thirty-seven counties returning two members each. The counties of Chester and Durham, which were counties palatine and under a semi-independent authority, did not come into the parliamentary system until a later date. Henry VIII brought in the Welsh counties. The Union with Scotland and with Ireland completed the list.

The history of the borough franchise is far more complicated. In the first place the writs addressed to the sheriff for returns to the early parliaments merely told him to provide for the return of two members for each city or borough in his county, and did not specify the places which were to be treated as boroughs. That was assumed to be known. The resultant uncertainty encouraged the exercise of discretion on the part of the sheriff. It had not yet been discovered that representation of a borough in parliament was a source of profit, local or personal, to the borough, or that it conferred personal advantage on its representative. On the contrary, when members were paid wages by their constituencies, and when places recognized as boroughs were taxed for subsidies at a higher rate than shires, representation in parliament was an onerous privilege. Towns often desired not to be represented, and probably made arrangements with the sheriff for this purpose. Later the tide turned, and in the sixteenth and seventeenth centuries the number of boroughs increased with great rapidity. The increase was effected in various ways. A borough which had ceased to return members might be revived in pursuance of a direction to the sheriff. The king might grant a charter giving a right of representation. Subsequently a resolution of the House of Commons sufficed for the right. The Tudor monarchs exercised freely their power of creating boroughs by charter. They used their parliaments and had to find means of controlling them. In the creation of 'pocket' or 'rotten' boroughs, Queen Elizabeth was probably the worst offender. She had much influence in her duchy of Cornwall, and many of the Cornish boroughs which obtained such a scandalous reputation in later times were created by her for the return of those whom the lords of her council would consider 'safe' men. The practice of creating new parliamentary boroughs by charter lessened under the Stuarts, and fell into desuetude after the reign of Charles II. The charter which he granted to Newark was the last royal charter conferring a parliamentary franchise.

There was no Act for the redistribution of borough seats until 1832. An interesting map prefixed to the first volume of Porritt's *Unreformed House of Commons* shows how borough representation stood at that date. A glance at this map discloses two features; first, the proportionately large number of boroughs on or near the coast from the Wash southwards and westwards to the Severn estuary, and next, the dense cluster of little boroughs in the extreme south-west. To some extent these features were survivals from an age of different social and economical conditions, from the time when the pulse of English life beat most strongly on the coasts, and when the growth of trade and manufacture had not yet filled up the central and northern regions. But the existence of many of the smaller boroughs was due to other reasons. Reference has been made already to the profuse creation of Cornish boroughs. In what was before 1918 the Liskeard division of Cornwall, a division returning one member, there were in 1832 nine boroughs returning eighteen members. In this region, and elsewhere, there were curious little twin boroughs, having no reason for their separate existence except the desire to multiply members. Such were West and East Looe, divided by a river which was spanned by a bridge of fifteen arches. Such also were Weymouth and Melcombe Regis, which were united for administrative purposes, but divided for purposes of parliamentary representation. In the early part of the eighteenth century these were controlled by the notorious borough-monger, Bubb Dodington, who atoned for his many misdeeds by leaving a diary in which they are recorded. Bramber and Steyning were close to each other in Sussex, and part of Bramber was in the centre of Steyning. Each returned two members. In Yorkshire, Aldborough and Boroughbridge were in the same parish, and about half a mile apart. The electors of Boroughbridge numbered sixty-five, those of Aldborough about fifty. Each returned two members at a time when Birmingham was not represented in parliament.

Whilst the selection and distribution of parliamentary boroughs was arbitrary, nothing could be more various, confused, or uncertain than the parliamentary franchise which they enjoyed. There was no general law regulating the franchise in boroughs. Everything depended on local custom and usage, settled or unsettled by the decisions of parliamentary committees, which turned upon personal and political considerations. The 'unreformed' boroughs as they stood before 1832 have been roughly divided into four groups. There were scot and lot and potwalloper boroughs, burgage boroughs, corporation boroughs, and freemen boroughs.

In the scot and lot group the franchise was, in theory, very democratic. Anyone who was liable to pay 'scot', or local dues, or to bear 'lot', that is to say, take his share in the burden of local offices, was entitled to the franchise. In later times liability to the poor rate was taken as a general test. At the time of the first Reform Act, Gatton, with 135 inhabitants, was a scot and lot borough. So, at the other end of the population scale, was Westminster. The potwalloper, or potwaller, who is treated as belonging to this group, was an ancient and picturesque person. As the syllables 'wallop' and 'wall' convey in Old English the meaning of boiling, we are to understand that he was a man who could boil a pot of his own, and was not dependent for his meals on anyone else. On the eve of an election a potwalloper might be seen spreading his board in front of his hovel, to show that he was entitled to the franchise. In burgage boroughs the right to vote depended on showing title to a house or piece of land by the form of tenure known as burgage tenure. In some cases residence was necessary, and the chimneys of burgage hovels were carefully preserved, as evidence of the possibility of residence. But the necessary period of residence might be short, and a single night might suffice. Coaches could be seen carrying down qualifying burdens on the eve of the poll.

In other cases residence was not necessary, or even possible. At Droitwich the qualification of an elector was being 'seised in fee of a small quantity of salt water arising out of a pit'. It was proved before a parliamentary committee that the pit had been dried up for more than forty years; but there were title deeds which could be produced by the voter at the poll. At Downton, in Wiltshire, one of the burgage tenements was in the middle of a watercourse. At Old Sarum, where ploughed fields gave seven votes which returned two members, there was no building, and a tent had to be erected for the shelter of the returning officer. Title deeds to qualifying property of this kind passed easily and rapidly from hand to hand as occasion required. Hence the class of 'snatchpaper' voters. A woman could not vote herself, but she could pass on her qualification temporarily to any man. At Westbury a widow's qualifying tenement was worth £100 to her in 1747.

For the mode in which an election might be conducted in a burgage borough Sir George Trevelyan's description of the first election of Charles James Fox may suffice. His father and uncle wanted to keep their boys steady, a difficult matter; so they clubbed together to find a borough. For Charles, who was then just nineteen, the two brothers

'selected Midhurst, the most comfortable of constituencies from the point of view of a representative; for the right of election rested in a few small holdings, on which no human being resided, distinguished among the pastures and the stubble that surrounded them by a large stone set up on end in the middle of each portion. These burgage tenures, as they were called, had all been bought up by a single proprietor, Viscount Montagu, who, when an election was in prospect, assigned a few of them to his servants, with instructions to nominate the members and then make back the property to their employer. This ceremony was performed in March, 1768, and the steward of the estate who acted as the returning officer, declared that Charles James Fox had been duly chosen as one of the burgesses for Midhurst, at a time when that young gentleman was still amusing himself in Italy.'

In the 'corporation boroughs' or 'close boroughs', the right to vote was restricted by charter to the members of what was called the governing body of the borough, a body very different in constitution and functions from the governing bodies created by the Municipal Corporations Act of 1835. They were usually self-elected, they were often non-resident, they were not responsible to anyone for the management of municipal affairs, and they existed, not primarily for the good administration of the borough, but as organizations for returning members to the House of Commons. In the eighteenth century they mostly fell into the hands of patrons, and, for a suitable consideration, returned the members nominated by their patrons. With the reform of parliament the reason for their existence ceased; the Act of 1835 followed speedily after the Act of 1832.

The freeman who exercised the parliamentary franchise in the eighteenth century was a different person from the freeman who voted in the thirteenth and fourteenth centuries; he belonged to a more restricted class. Freedom of the borough, membership of the general corporation which constituted the borough, as distinguished from its governing body, might be acquired in various ways—by birth, by marriage, by real or nominal service as apprenticeship to some freeman in his craft or trade, by gift or purchase. In London, membership of one of the City livery companies such as the Mercers or Goldsmiths was necessary. Where freedom came by marriage, it was practically a dower to the freeman's daughter, and had a very tangible pecuniary value at election times. 'I have heard that in former days', wrote a town clerk of Bristol, 'the prospect of an election would bring hesitating or lagging swains to a sense of the desirability of prompt action.' There were honorary freemen and non-resident freemen, both having votes. The tendency of parliamentary action was to restrict the class of freemen, for the representation of a borough with numerous freemen was an expensive luxury. On the other hand, it might be convenient to swamp the existing body of electors. At Bristol, in 1812, 1,720 freemen were admitted with a view to an election in the autumn of that year.

Under the electoral system as it worked before 1832 a small number of powerful and wealthy men controlled all the elections. Not that the House of Commons was uninfluenced by public opinion. Any great wave of feeling or opinion was sure to reach the House and to produce effects there. The counties were more independent than the boroughs, and the larger boroughs sometimes had views of their own as to the way in which their members should vote. But the number of pocket boroughs, whose members were expected to vote as their patrons told them, was very large. John Wilson Croker, who knew the House of Commons during the first quarter of the last century as well as anyone, put the members returned by patrons at 276 out of 658. Before the union with Ireland increased the number of members by 100, the proportion was probably greater, for the number of nomination seats in Ireland did not exceed twenty. It has been estimated that from about 1760 to 1832 nearly one-half of the members of the House of Commons owed their seats to patrons. Gladstone once eulogized nomination boroughs as a means of bringing young men of promise into the house; Bagehot went so far as to describe them as an organ for specialized political thought. But a study of electoral statistics and parliamentary history tends to show that the young men of promise who were given a comparatively free hand were rare, and that the tie between the nominated member and his patron was much less romantic and more prosaic and practical than as conceived by Bagehot. A nominee member was usually expected to obey his patron's orders, and to study his interests. In 1810 a younger brother, who had been put into parliament by his senior, was reprimanded for neglecting the family interests.

'As to my being justifiable in thus abandoning the interests of my family, after all the money that has been spent to bring me into parliament [he writes in reply], I have only to answer that the money so spent has, I think, been well spent. Your lord lieutenancy and Peter's receiver-generalship have been the consequence. In point of pecuniary advantage to the family the receiver-generalship pays more than the interest on the capital sunk.'

The seat was a good family investment. For patronship, discreetly used, brought honours and lucrative sinecures. Sir James Lowther returned nine members, the 'Lowther ninepins'; he obtained a peerage, and successive steps in the peerage. George Selwyn returned two members for Ludgershall, and was sometimes able to return one of the members for Gloucester.

'He was [says Sir George Trevelyan] at one and the same time Surveyor-General of Crown Lands, which he never surveyed; Registrar of Chancery at Barbadoes, which he never visited; and Surveyor of the Meltings and Clerk of the Irons in the Mint, where he showed himself once a week in order to eat a dinner which he ordered, but for which the nation paid.'

The payments to constituents, in the form of cash or office, were smaller but more numerous. Posts in the Customs and Excise were freely used. Bossinney, a little fishing village in the north of Cornwall, was once a borough. When the Act of 1782 disfranchised revenue officers, it reduced the voters at Bossinney to a single elector.

If a candidate could not find a patron, or did not wish to be dependent on a patron, he had to buy a seat. Many of the reformers, men such as Burdett, Romilly, and Hume, had to buy their seats. Throughout the eighteenth and the early part of the nineteenth century seats were freely and openly bought and sold. They were even advertised for sale, as church livings used to be. The price of seats went up rapidly during the latter half of the eighteenth century, especially when East Indian nabobs entered the market. The Government of course took a large share in these transactions, and Treasury boroughs were kept for those who were wanted on the Treasury Bench, or who could be counted on to give a safe vote in its neighbourhood. Bargains were struck for dividing the cost between the Treasury and the member.

'Mr. Legge [wrote Lord North in 1774 to Robinson, his chief election manager] can afford only £400. If he comes in for Lostwithiel, he will cost the public 2,000 guineas. Gascoyne should have the refusal of Tregony if he will pay £1,000, but I do not see why we should bring him in cheaper than any other servant of the Crown. If he will not pay, he must give way to Mr. Best or Mr. Peachy.'

The Whig administration of 1806 adopted a more economical method. It bought seats cheap and sold them dear, and thus saved money for the public. A seat could be bought for a parliament, or hired for a term of years like a country house. Prices varied much, according to place and time, but between 1812 and 1832 the ordinary price of a seat bought for a parliament is said to have been between £5,000 and £6,000.

Without concrete illustrations such as have been given it is impossible to realize in the twentieth century the working of the electoral system which prevailed before the Age of Reform. The details are sordid and unpleasant. But it must be remembered that on these sordid foundations was built a government whose strength and stability won the admiration and envy of Europe. Burke, and the other conservatives of his time, Whig and Tory, had solid reasons for their convictions when they resisted all changes in the electoral system under which they lived.

'Our representation [wrote Burke] has been found perfectly adequate to all the purposes for which a representation of the people can be desired or devised. I defy the enemies of our constitution to show the contrary.'

It is true that he wrote these words in his later days, under the terrifying influence of the French Revolution; but they represented the views which he had always held about the franchise. According to him, the variety of franchise in the boroughs, and the mode in which the constituencies were controlled, roughly represented the various interests of the nation and its ruling forces. The king and his ministers had to rule; the discordant elements in the country and the constitution had to be kept together. It was difficult to see how any form of government could be maintained except by the employment of methods such as have been described above. The ruling class of the eighteenth century were coarse and corrupt, but they were capable and courageous. They made great blunders, they were blind and indifferent to great evils, but they weathered terrible storms.

Into the various causes which brought about the Reform Act of 1832 this is not the place to enter. The generation of statesmen who had carried on the great war had passed away. The governments of the later 'twenties were weak and unstable. The reaction against the excesses of the French Revolution was losing its force. Bentham's principles, which were hostile to a privileged class, and made in the long run for democracy, were being popularized by such men as James Mill and Francis Place. But, above all, there was grave and growing discontent on the part of the middle class with the existing state of things, with their exclusion from political power, and with the practical grievances which, in their opinion, were due to that exclusion. They felt that the House of Commons was not in touch with the country at large, that it failed to represent the most vital and growing elements in the nation. The Reform Bill was introduced by Whig aristocrats, but it was the middle class that carried it through.

The Reform Act of 1832 made a radical change in the system of elections and in the constitution of the House of Commons. It redistributed seats, it simplified and rationalized the franchise, it established registers of electors.

The number of seats in the House of Commons had been rapidly increased under the Tudors, less rapidly under the Stuarts. Thus Henry VIII created 38 seats, including the Welsh constituencies, and Elizabeth 62. The union with Scotland in 1707 added 45 members, that with Ireland in 1801 added 100. In 1832 the total number of members was 658. Five of the English boroughs returned single members. Yorkshire sent four members, having gained two by the disfranchisement of Grampound in 1821. The City of London also sent four members. With these exceptions, each constituency in England returned two members, the number fixed for the earliest English parliaments. Each of the twelve counties and twelve boroughs in Wales returned a single member.

The Act of 1832 materially altered the distribution of seats. It disfranchised in England fifty-six boroughs absolutely, and thirty-one to the extent of depriving each of one member. The seats taken from the boroughs were given to counties and large towns.

The alterations made by the Act in the parliamentary franchise were numerous and important. In the counties it preserved the old forty-shilling freehold franchise, with some limitations, and it added some new classes of voters. It enfranchised four main classes: (1) the £10 copyholders, (2) the £10 long leaseholders, (3) the £50 short leaseholders, and (4) the £50 occupiers.

Into the boroughs the Act introduced one uniform franchise, the £10 occupation franchise which was in force until 1867. The Act preserved some of the old qualifications, but placed them under restrictions intended to guard against their abuse. Freemen were still entitled to vote, as such, in certain boroughs. But the old qualifications had in most cases been made unimportant by the extension of the occupation franchise.

Finally, the Act introduced the machinery of parliamentary registration, substantially on its existing lines. Since 1832 a qualification to vote entitles a man to be placed on the register, not to vote. Unless he is on the register he is not entitled to vote. If he is on the register he is presumably entitled to vote.

Separate Reform Acts for Scotland and Ireland, framed on the same general lines as the English Act, were passed in the same year. They gave three additional members to Scotland, and three to Ireland, but the total number of seats for the United Kingdom was not altered.

The Reform Act of 1832 did not realize the hopes of its friends or the fears of its foes. Like most English Acts, it was based on compromise, not on abstract principle. Its objects were to remedy the most obvious grievances, to remove the most glaring anomalies and abuses. In dealing with distribution, it did not parcel out the country into equal, or approximately equal, electoral districts. It merely shifted seats, with some regard to the population and character of the places to be represented. It preserved old franchises, and superimposed new franchises upon them. It did not introduce and was not intended to introduce, democracy. It gave electoral power, in the counties, to the landholders with a few large farmers; in the towns, to the great middle class. The borough electorate in England and Wales was increased by about 100,000. There was no finality about the Act. It was a step forward, suggesting further steps at a later date. It did not put an end to bribery, corruption, or the exercise of undue influence. But the opportunities for these practices were made fewer and less easy, and the practices became less flagrant and universal.

Thus the Act of 1832 was not the product of, and did not effect, a revolution. But its importance, political, social, and economical, cannot be exaggerated. It was one of the great landmarks of English history.

The reformed House of Commons reflected the virtues of the middle class, and their weaknesses. The influence of the middle class preponderated, as under the contemporary bourgeois rule of Louis Philippe. But Louis Philippe's régime died of corruption and stagnation in 1848, whilst the English chartism of that year shook neither parliament nor the throne. For the British parliament had justified its existence in its renovated form, and had accomplished some great things. It had reformed the poor law; it had reformed municipal government; it had reformed the fiscal system.

It is in the sphere of legislation that the difference between the unreformed and the reformed House of Commons is most marked. It is impossible to emphasize too strongly the enormous change which the Reform Act of 1832 introduced into the character of English legislation, or the complete contrast between the legislation which preceded and the legislation which followed that date. The eighteenth century and the first two decades of the nineteenth century were prolific of legislation, but it was of an ephemeral character. The parliament of the eighteenth century passed many laws which would now be classed as local Acts, for authorizing the construction of roads, canals, and bridges, and was never tired of regulating, after its lights, the conditions of labour, the conduct of trades and industries, and the relief of the poor. But it created no new institutions. It is after the Reform Act that we get the series of Acts which began with remodelling the poor law and municipal corporations, and which have completely altered the framework of our central and local government. And from the same time dates that special responsibility of the Government for legislation which is now so marked a feature of the parliament at Westminster. Sir Charles Wood, afterwards Lord Halifax, first took his seat in the House of Commons in 1828, and, when talking to Mr. Nassau Senior in 1855, he dwelt on the changed attitude of the Government towards legislation.

'When I was first in parliament [he said] twenty-seven years ago, the functions of the Government were chiefly executive. Changes in our laws were proposed by independent members, and carried, not as party questions, by their combined action on both sides. Now, when an independent member brings forward a subject, it is not to propose himself a measure, but to call to it the attention of the Government. All the House joins in declaring that the present state of the law is abominable, and in requiring the Government to provide a remedy. As soon as the Government has obeyed, and proposed one, they all oppose it. Our defects as legislators, which is not our business, damage us as administrators, which is our business.'

This was a natural expression to fall from the lips of an experienced statesman who had lived through the change, and had not quite lost the habit of mind which preceded it. And one still hears from private members regrets for the time when their predecessors enjoyed greater freedom of legislative action, and denunciations of Government encroachments on their legislative opportunities. But the change has been inevitable. The great demand for new laws, especially laws which create, remodel, and regulate administrative machinery, and the importance, difficulty, and complexity of the legislative measures required, necessarily lessen the share of the private member in the initiation and passing of laws, and increase the responsibility of the Government for the work of legislation.

The great outburst of parliamentary activity immediately after 1832 was naturally followed by a reaction, and there were periods of failure and inactivity, legislative and administrative. Walter Bagehot has given an inimitable description of the Palmerstonian House of Commons, as it stood in the years 1865 and 1866. No one could hit off more neatly the habits and ways of that House, or was more fully aware that its leader, who had been in political harness long before 1832, represented traditions of government which were passing away, and ought to pass away. Palmerston in his later years opposed a steady and usually an effective resistance to all changes, and his last ministry, from 1859 to 1866, was a period of exceptional barrenness in legislation. But when, after 1867, Bagehot wrote the preface to the second edition of his book on the English Constitution, it is evident that he had misgivings about the effect of the Act of 1867; one suspects that he looked back to the Palmerstonian period as the golden age of what was, in his opinion, the best of all governments, a safe, sober, cautious middle-class government.

The Reform Act of 1832 had shown the possibility of making changes in an electoral system which was venerable, and was venerated, by reason of its antiquity. It suggested and paved the way for further changes.

There was, as has been said above, no finality in its provisions. The forty-shilling freeholder came down from the Middle Ages. But there was nothing venerable or sacrosanct about the £50 leaseholder or the £10 occupier. If £10, why not some other figure?

Disraeli was the first minister who was bold enough to propose dispensing with all tests of rental or rating, and to offer the borough franchise to householders as such. The history of the Representation of the People Act 1867 is well known; its inner side was revealed many years ago in Lord Malmesbury's indiscreet *Memoirs of an Ex-Minister*. The Bill of 1867, as introduced, while conferring the household franchise, surrounded it with safeguards. The householder was required to have resided for two years, and to have paid his rates personally. A householder paying twenty shillings in direct taxation was to have a second vote, and there were some special franchises, as in previous Bills. But the Government which introduced the Bill was in a minority in the House of Commons, and all these safeguards disappeared in committee. The period of residence was reduced to one year. The second vote and the fancy franchises disappeared. After a long battle over the 'compound householder' (the man whose rates are paid for him by his landlord), compounding was abolished, and all householders were to be rated in person. But this was found so inconvenient that, two years later, compounding was restored, and personal payment of rates ceased to be a necessary qualification for being registered as a voter. Lastly, £10 lodgers were admitted to the vote. Thus the measure was completely transformed, and it has been estimated that the number of persons enfranchised was increased from about

100,000 to about two millions. These were the changes made by the Act of 1867 in the borough franchise. Those which it made in the county franchise were less important. It reduced the £10 qualification, for copyholders and leaseholders, to £5. And it added a £12 rateable occupation franchise which practically took the place of the £50 rental franchise.

The Act of 1867 enfranchised the urban working man as the Act of 1832 had enfranchised the mainly urban middle class. Its effects made themselves apparent, specially in the changed attitude of the legislature towards trade unions, and generally in the great outburst of legislative activity during Gladstone's first ministry, a period as fertile in legislation as the period immediately preceding 1867 had been barren.

Among the Acts passed during that ministry was the Ballot Act 1872 which introduced into parliamentary elections the system of election by secret ballot, a fundamental principle not seriously offended by the Act of 1933 which allows a blind voter to be assisted by a relative or friend. Vote by ballot had been one of the famous 'six points' of the Charter of 1848, and proposals for establishing it had been annually introduced by private members; but, before the ministry of 1869, it had never been supported or proposed by the Government. The Act was not passed without a long and hard fight, and then only as an experimental measure, to remain in force for one year only, unless renewed. For fifty-five years it was renewed annually by the Expiring Laws Continuance Act of each year, and it was not until the whole system of parliamentary representation was radically changed by the Representation of the People Act 1918 that the Ballot Act was given a place on the statute book as a permanent measure. The Ballot Act put an end to the venerable ceremonies of election at the old county court and the hustings, and, incidentally, by altering the form of the writ for elections, removed the distinction between knights, citizens, and burgesses, grouping them all as 'members'.

A further stage in the history of the reform of parliamentary elections was marked by the Representation of the People Act 1884 and by the Act for the Redistribution of Seats which followed in 1885. The Act of 1884 dealt only with the franchise, leaving the distribution of seats untouched. It extended to the counties the household and lodger franchise which the Act of 1867 had conferred on the boroughs. It also remodelled the occupation qualification, making the occupation of any land or tenement of a clear yearly value of £10 a qualification both in boroughs and in counties. And it created a new form of franchise, called the service franchise, intended to meet some cases not quite covered by the householder or the lodger vote. The Act increased the electorate by forty per cent, and its most important effect was the enfranchisement of the rural working man. The Act of 1867 had given the vote to the working man in the town. The Act of 1884 gave it to the working man in the country, the agricultural labourer and his like. It was soon afterwards that the famous 'three acres and a cow' made their appearance on the parliamentary scene.

The House of Lords refused to pass the Act of 1884 unless it was accompanied by a measure for the redistribution of seats. The difference between the two Houses was ended by a compromise, in pursuance of which, after an adjournment, a Bill was brought in which became law as the Redistribution of Seats Act of 1885. The terms of the Bill were settled, during the adjournment, by an arrangement between the chiefs of the two parties; so numerous and conflicting were the interests involved that without some such agreement the Bill could not have become law.

The Act of 1885, though to some extent a compromise, was drawn on bolder lines than its predecessors, and was based on the general principle of equal electoral districts each returning a single member. The proportion of one seat for every 54,000 people was roughly taken as the basis of representation. In order to adapt this principle to the then existing system with the least possible change, boroughs with less than 15,000 inhabitants were disfranchised altogether, and became, for electoral purposes, a part of the county in which they were situated. Boroughs with more than 15,000 and less than 50,000 inhabitants were allowed to retain, or if previously unrepresented were given, one member each: those with more than 50,000 and less than 165,000, two members; those above 165,000, three members, with an additional member for every 50,000 people more. The same general principle was followed in the counties.

The boroughs which had previously elected two members, and retained that number, remained single constituencies for the election of those two members. Of these boroughs there were twenty-three, and these, with the City of London, and the three universities of Oxford, Cambridge, and Dublin, made the twenty-seven cases of constituencies returning two members. All the other constituencies were single-member districts, a result which was brought about by dividing the counties, boroughs with more than two members, and the new boroughs with only two members, into separate electoral divisions, each with its own distinctive name.

The total number of members was increased from 658 to 670, the number at which it stood until 1918.

The Representation of the People Act 1918 was founded on the report of a conference between members of both Houses, which sat under the chairmanship of Mr. Speaker Lowther, afterwards Lord Ullswater. It made sweeping and fundamental changes in the law as to the franchise, the registration of electors, the methods of election, and the distribution of seats. It gave votes to women. It abolished the old parliamentary franchises and substituted a simple franchise based either on residence or on the occupation of business premises. A man was to get the parliamentary vote if he had for six months resided or occupied premises either in the same constituency or in another constituency in the same or a contiguous parliamentary borough or county. A woman was to get the parliamentary vote if she had attained the age of thirty, and if either she or her husband was on the register of electors at local elections. Thus the wife of a peer could have the vote though her husband could not. The university franchise was retained with an extension to persons who had taken any degree other than an honorary degree, and the number of university constituencies was increased. A woman got the university franchise if she had attained the age of thirty and had either taken the degree qualifying a man for a vote or kept the residence and passed the examinations entitling to such a degree.

It was estimated that the new law increased the

number of electors in the United Kingdom by about eight millions.

Before we come to more recent changes in the franchise we may note some other important modifications of electoral law made by the Act of 1918.

At a general election all elections, except for university seats, were to be held on the same day, and an elector was not to vote in more than two constituencies.

The general demand for payment of the official expenses of candidates was met by providing that all the returning officers' expenses at a parliamentary election, other than a university election, were (subject to a maximum fixed by the Treasury) to be paid out of the Exchequer. But every candidate had, on nomination, to deposit with the returning officer a sum of £150, which was to be repaid to a successful candidate on his taking his seat and the oath, and to be forfeited if the candidate failed to obtain one-eighth of the votes polled. The object was to guard against 'freak candidates'.

The parliamentary register was adapted to the shortened period of qualification by providing for half-yearly instead of yearly registers, though in 1926, as a measure of economy, the yearly register was reinstated.

Revising barristers, who used to be appointed to deal locally with the claims of would-be voters and the challenges to voters already registered, were abolished in 1918. Henceforth there was to be for each registration area a registration officer, whose decisions would be subject to appeal to a county court.

Another change effected in 1918 was the elaborate provision for recording the votes of absent voters. They may vote either by post or by proxy, but proxy voting is only allowed where a ballot paper dispatched on the day of nomination cannot reach the returning officer by post before the counting of the votes, which is for this purpose postponed until some days after the election. These provisions were intended mainly for naval and military voters, but are not confined to that class of voters or limited to war-time. Any person is entitled to be placed on the absent voter's list and to vote as an absent voter if he satisfies the registration officer that by reason of the nature of his occupation, service, or employment, he may be debarred from voting at a poll. Thus the provisions are available, not only for the soldier and sailor, but for such classes of the population as merchant seamen, commercial travellers, and diplomatic representatives. The right to vote by proxy is, however, confined to naval and military voters afloat or in proxy areas, and to merchant seamen, pilots, and fishermen.

The Speaker's Conference recommended in 1917 the adoption of the principles of proportional representation and of the alternative vote. The object of proportional representation is the protection of minorities. The alternative vote is an Australian invention intended to take the place of the second ballot which found favour with earlier reformers, and to secure the return of a member representing the majority in the case of a three-cornered contest. Both these principles were adopted in the Bill based on the recommendations of the Conference. But the alternative vote, after a precarious existence in the House of Commons, was killed in the House of Lords. Proportional representation was rejected in the Commons, but by a proposal made in the House of Lords and accepted in the other House, commissioners were appointed to prepare a scheme for applying the principle to 100 constituencies, and the scheme was to take effect if approved by both Houses of Parliament. A scheme was prepared, but was rejected by the House of Commons. Proportional representation, as applied to parliamentary elections, is at present confined to university elections, for which it is not well adapted. But it was applied to elections to education authorities in Scotland and was tried for a time in local elections in Ireland.

When the Irish Free State (now Eire) was constituted in 1922, Southern Ireland ceased to be represented in the House of Commons. Thenceforth the House consisted of 615 members, namely 492 for England, 36 for Wales, 74 for Scotland, and 13 for Northern Ireland.

In 1928 the Representation of the People (Equal Franchise) Act assimilated the franchises for men and women and thereby increased the electorate to something over 28,000,000.

For the general election which took place in 1945 extemporized arrangements were made. The Parliament elected in 1935 should have come to an end when its five-year term was up in 1940. By the latter date the nation had other things to think about and was unwilling that domestic politics should disturb its concentration. With the elasticity which is characteristic of the British Constitution the five-year period was annually prolonged by a series of short Acts until 1945. A general election, however, could not be postponed indefinitely, and in 1943 the prospects of victory in Europe justified an examination of difficulties due to the lapse of the annual revision of the register and to the war-time shifting of population. A Speaker's Conference proceeded with proposals for the redistribution of seats (including transitional arrangements for new constituencies) and Parliament decided to experiment temporarily with a voters' list compiled from the material made available by the National Registration Acts, under which food rationing had been successfully organized. Owing to various causes the experimental list omitted the names of many voters who were qualified; the temporary method seemed to be no adequate substitute for the peace-time lists revised by annual house-to-house inquiries.

For the 1945 election the transitional revision of constituencies brought the total number of seats up to 640. There were three registers, one based on residence as recorded under the emergency system of identity cards, another for those who claimed a business qualification, and a third for the armed forces, merchant seamen, and oversea war-workers. With so many voters serving abroad special provision was made for voting by post as well as by proxy. Steps were taken later to replace these improvized arrangements and also to plan the redistribution of seats on a basis of one-member constituencies consisting of approximately 50,000 voters each.

Something may now be said about the qualification of members as distinguished from voters. A residential qualification was imposed in the fifteenth century, but soon became obsolete, and was formally repealed, as such, in the eighteenth century. By the legislation of that century a property qualification was required, but it was easily evaded and was abolished by a private member's Act in 1858. Oaths of allegiance and oaths imposing religious tests in various forms and degrees of stringency were introduced in the sixteenth and seventeenth centuries; and their modification and abolition, and the steps by which Roman Catholics, Jews, and others obtained admission into the House of Commons, form an interesting chapter in parliamentary history. The simple oath or affirmation now required, raising no issue of religious belief or unbelief, merely promises allegiance to the Crown. Two Northern Ireland constituencies were disfranchised from 1935 to 1945 because their chosen representatives refused to make the promise.

An Act passed at the end of 1918, before the general election of that year, enabled women not merely to vote for but to sit in the House of Commons. Several women were candidates, but only one (Countess Markievicz) obtained a majority of votes, and she was disqualified for election. Lady Astor, by her success at a subsequent by-election, was the first woman to sit in the House.

Clergy of the Established Church or the Roman Catholic Church, and ministers of the Church of Scotland, may not be elected. Subject to these disqualifications and others arising from peerage, holding of office, Government contracts, bankruptcy, insanity, corrupt practices at elections, and conviction of treason or felony, every British subject who is of full age is eligible to the House of Commons. A peer of the United Kingdom or of Scotland is not eligible, but a peer of Ireland, unless he be one of the dwindling band of representative peers (of whom more will be said in a later chapter) is eligible for any seat except one in Northern Ireland. Where a member of the House of Commons is described as a lord, he is either an Irish peer, or more frequently, a commoner holding a courtesy title as son of a peer.

About disqualification by office something more must be said. After the restoration of Charles II, and indeed until the end of the seventeenth century, there was much jealousy of the presence in parliament of persons holding office under the king. It was feared that, through his officers, the king would be able to exercise undue influence over parliamentary proceedings, and an Act was passed which made the holding of all such offices incompatible with a seat in the House of Commons. Fortunately this Act was repealed before it came into operation. If it had remained law, it would not only have crippled the House of Commons by concentrating political leadership in the House of Lords, but would also have made our present system of government impossible because parliamentary control of the executive is not properly ensured unless a certain quota of responsible ministers can sit in the House of Commons and be challenged there in respect of the conduct of their departments.

To sum up briefly a far too complicated series of laws, there are certain non-ministerial offices, such as judgeships and posts in the permanent civil service, which are naturally treated as incompatible with membership of the House of Commons. Because most of the government departments must be represented in parliament, it is usual to have two ministers in each of such departments; if one of the pair sits in the House of Commons, it will often be convenient that the other should sit in the House of Lords. As the Succession to the Crown Act 1707 contemplated when it instituted its technical rules disqualifying the holders of offices of profit under the Crown from membership of the House of Commons, there must be some limit on the number of ministers sitting in that House. Until quite recently there were many ministerial offices the acceptance of which did not disqualify the holder from membership but did compel him to vacate his seat and offer himself for re-election. In 1919 the Re-election of Ministers Act made this process unnecessary if the member were appointed to the office within nine months from a general election. Thus, after a general election, a member had a 'close time' during which he could accept a political office without running the gauntlet of re-election. In 1926 an amending Act abolished the necessity for re-election altogether.

The evidence of election is the return sent to the Clerk of the Crown in Chancery (a high official who is also permanent secretary to the Lord Chancellor) by the returning officer at the election. If the validity of an election is disputed, the question is tried and decided by election judges appointed by, and from among members of, the High Court.

A member cannot resign his seat, but, if he wishes to retire from parliament, he takes advantage of the old disqualifying statutes by asking for appointment to some ancient office to which nominal duties and emoluments are attached. The office usually selected for this purpose is that of steward or bailiff of His Majesty's three Chiltern Hundreds of Stoke, Desborough, and Burnham, in the county of Bucks. Acceptance of the Chiltern Hundreds is the door by which a member escapes when he wishes to retire from parliament before a general election. If two members find themselves in this position simultaneously, the stewardship of the manor of Northstead usually provides the second appointment.

Members of the House of Commons, other than those in receipt of ministerial salaries, now receive a salary of £1,000 a year. It is not exempt from income tax except in so far as the member, like any other citizen who holds an office, can deduct expenses wholly, exclusively, and necessarily incurred in the performance of his office. Members also have free first-class travelling facilities to and from their constituencies and, since 1945, to and from their homes when the House is sitting. An annual payment of £400 was first authorized by a resolution of the House in 1911, to enable a member, in Mr. Lloyd George's words, to maintain himself comfortably and honourably, but not luxuriously. It was increased to £600 in 1937, and to £1,000 in 1946. The authority rests not on a permanent statute but on an annual vote confirmed by the Appropriation Act of the year. A subsistence allowance is granted to members when travelling upon the business of the House. The Ministers of the Crown Act 1937 which fixed the salaries of the Prime Minister and the holders of the major administrative offices of State and parliamentary under-secretaries, broke fresh ground by providing a salary for the Leader of the Opposition. A Treasury decision, announced in 1947, allowed the Prime Minister to deduct for expenses four-fifths of his salary of £5,000. A member's salary runs from the time at which he takes the oath of allegiance or makes the equivalent affirmation. Under an Act of 1939 a small deduction is made from salaries for contribution to a House of Commons Members' Fund for a pensions scheme.

CHAPTER III

THE MAKING OF LAWS

THE BUSINESS of the House of Commons may be divided into three branches, legislative, financial, critical. The House makes laws with the concurrence of the House of Lords and the king. It grants money for the public service, specifies the purposes to which that money is to be appropriated, imposes taxes and authorizes loans. By means of questions and discussions, it criticizes and controls the action of the king's ministers, and of the executive Government of which they are at the head.

Let us begin with the work of making laws. The law of this country is commonly classified as falling under two heads, the common law and the statute law. The common law may for present purposes be described as the law which is based on custom and usage as declared and expounded by judges. The statute law is the law which is made by the legislature and is to be found in Acts of Parliament, or, as they are also called, the statutes of the realm. There are other distinctions and refinements with which we need not concern ourselves here. It is with the making of statute law that Parliament is concerned. The gradual change in the form of parliamentary legislation, by which legislation on petition was transformed into legislation by Bill, has been described in our first chapter.

In dealing with the work of legislation, as conducted under modern rules of procedure, it may be convenient to begin by describing, very briefly, the stages through which a Bill, that is, a project of law, or a proposed law, must pass before it obtains the king's assent, becomes an Act of Parliament, and acquires the force of law. We will suppose that it is a Public Bill, that is, a Bill for the alteration of the general law, as distinguished from a Private Bill, the nature of which will be explained later, and that it makes its start in the House of Commons, not in our first chapter.

In sessions in war-time or other abnormal periods the House of Commons has ordered that no Public Bills other than Government Bills be introduced. Subject to that temporary restriction, any member of the House may introduce a Bill into that House, or move the House for leave to introduce it. Formerly this motion for leave, which was rarely refused, was the preliminary step for introduction of a Bill, and the old practice was frequently followed in the case of the more important measures introduced by the Government, and sometimes in the case of Bills introduced by private members. But, under an alteration of rules made in 1902, any member may now present a Bill, after giving formal notice of his intention to do so. If he has obtained the requisite leave, or given the requisite notice, the Speaker, at the proper time, calls his name, and thus invites him to present his Bill. He does so by bringing to the table of the House, where the clerks sit, a document which is supposed to be his Bill, but which is really a 'dummy' or sheet of paper, supplied to him at the Public Bill Office, and containing the title of the Bill, the member's name, and the names of any other members who wish to appear as supporting him or joining with him in presenting the Bill. The clerk at the table reads out the title of the Bill, and it is then supposed to have been read a first time. A formal order is made for printing it, and a day is fixed for its second reading. There was a time when these so-called 'readings' were realities. The Speaker would explain, from notes or a 'breviate' supplied to him, the general nature of the proposals to be brought before the House, and the Bill itself would probably be read in full, at later stages, by the clerk at the table of the House. Nowadays the 'readings' are merely stages in the progress of a Bill through the house. The first reading is a mere formality. Later when the question is put that the Bill be read a second time, an opportunity is afforded for discussing its general principles as distinguished from its details. If the House signifies its approval of these principles, the Bill is deemed to have been read a second time, and then follows what is called the committee stage. Under a Standing Order, when a Bill has been read a second time it is sent upstairs to one of the Standing Committees on Bills, unless it falls under certain exceptions, or unless the House makes an order that it be considered by some other kind of committee.

Though they were suspended from the outbreak of war in 1939 till March 1945, there have normally been six of these Standing Committees. One of them is for the consideration of Public Bills relating exclusively to Scotland, and must include all the members representing Scottish constituencies. The others are constituted by the Committee of Selection, which is one of the committees appointed for each session by the House; the same Committee of Selection also reinforces the committee on Scottish Bills by adding to it some other members. The minimum number of each standing committee is forty, and the quorum for business is twenty. Notwithstanding the heavy demands thereby made upon members' time and upon staff and accommodation, the 1945 parliament experimentally removed the limit on the number of Standing Committees (and reduced the quorum) in the hope of expediting progress with a heavy programme of post-war legislation.

If a Bill does not go to a Standing Committee, it usually goes to what is called a committee of the whole House. This is really the House itself, transacting its business in a less formal manner, with the Speaker's chair vacant, and sitting under the presidency of a chairman, who occupies the chair at the table which is occupied by the Clerk of the House when the Speaker is present. These so-called committees of the whole House, corresponding to what are called 'committees of the whole' in the United States, came into existence at the beginning of the seventeenth century. The more important Bills were then sent to large committees, and, as it was difficult to obtain attendance at these committees, orders were often made that any member who wished might attend. These orders grew into a general practice. It is said also that the House of that day did not place complete confidence in its Speaker, whom it regarded as the agent and nominee of the king, and that it preferred to conduct its deliberations in his absence. So it came to pass that what is called a committee of the whole House is the same body of persons as the House itself, sitting in the same place, with slightly different formalities and procedure.

Before the rule was changed in 1907, all Bills went after second reading to a committee of the whole House, unless the House ordered otherwise. Now the presumption is reversed, and all Bills, except special classes, go to a Standing Committee unless the House orders otherwise. But the Finance Bill and other money Bills of the year must go to a committee of the whole House, and objection is sometimes taken when it is proposed to send to a Standing Committee any of the more important Bills or any very controversial Bill, for, notwithstanding the change of rules, there are members who still hold that every member of the House ought to have an opportunity of taking part in the discussion of the detailed provisions of these Bills.

When a Bill is before a Standing Committee or a committee of the whole House, the committee goes through the Bill clause by clause, discussing any amendments that may be proposed, determining as to each clause, how, if at all, it should be amended, and whether in its original or amended form it should stand part of the Bill, and then whether any new clauses should be added. In the case of important and controversial Bills these debates may last over many days or weeks, and the notices of amendments to be proposed fill many pages of the parliamentary notice papers. When the discussion is finished, and the whole Bill has been gone through, the chairman of the committee makes a simple report to the Speaker and the House, merely stating whether the Bill has been amended or not.

In some cases a Bill, instead of going to a Standing Committee or to a committee of the whole House, is sent to a small select committee, or to a joint committee of both Houses. These cases are comparatively rare, and the reason for adopting this course usually is that it is desired to summon witnesses and take evidence as to the expediency and effect of the provisions of the Bill. Committees of this kind usually make special reports, stating their reasons and conclusions, but Bills considered by them have to be considered subsequently by a committee of the whole House.

After the committee stage follows the report stage. The House, sitting formally with the Speaker in the chair, considers the Bill as reported to it by the committee, and discusses and determines whether any further alterations or additions should be made.

The final stage in the House of Commons is the third reading. At this stage only formal or verbal alterations are allowed. The House considers the Bill as a whole, and determines whether, in its opinion, the measure ought or ought not to become law.

When a Bill has passed through all its stages in the House of Commons, it is sent up with a message to the House of Lords, to pass through its several stages there, stages which correspond, with some differences of detail, to those in the House of Commons. The Lords may reject the Bill or may amend it, but, as will be explained hereafter, they have no power to amend a Finance or other money Bill. If the Lords amend a Bill they send it back to the Commons with a message requesting the concurrence of the Commons in their amendments. Should the two Houses differ, informal negotiations take place between the friends and the opponents or critics of the Bill, and amendments and counter-amendments may pass to and fro between the two Houses until an agreement is arrived at. But if no agreement can be arranged, the Bill drops, that is to say, fails to become law, for, except in pursuance of the Parliament Act, 1911, a Bill cannot be presented for the royal assent until the concurrence of both Houses has been obtained. The life of a Bill is for one session only. If a Bill is not either passed or withdrawn by its promoters before the end of the session, it lapses or becomes a dead letter, and, if the proposals are to be proceeded with in the next or a subsequent session, there must be a new Bill.

When a Bill has been passed by both Houses, or in accordance with the Parliament Act, 1911, the final stage is the royal assent. This assent is given periodically to batches of Bills, as they are passed, the largest batch being usually at the end of the session. The traditional ceremony dates from Plantagenet times, and takes place in the House of Lords. The king is represented by Lords Commissioners, who sit in front of the throne, arrayed in scarlet robes and little cocked hats. Business in both Houses is interrupted. At the bar of the House stands the Speaker of the House of Commons, who has been summoned from that House. Behind him stand such members of the House of Commons as have followed him through the lobbies. A clerk of the House of Lords reads out, in a sonorous voice, the royal commission which authorizes the assent to be given. The Clerk of the Crown at one side of the table reads out the title of each Bill. The Clerk of the Parliaments on the other side, making profound obeisances, pronounces the Norman-French formula by which the king's assent is signified; 'Little Peddlington Electricity Supply Act,' '*Le Roy le veult*'. Between the two voices six centuries lie.

Since the time of Queen Anne no English king or queen has ever refused assent to a Bill. For, under the modern constitutional rule, the king must, in matters such as this, act in accordance with the advice of his ministers, and his ministers can manage to prevent any Bills which, in their opinion, ought not to become law from reaching the stage at which his assent is required.

A Bill cannot be introduced except by a member of

parliament; any member can introduce a Bill, unless its main object is to create a charge on public funds. When a minister of the Crown introduces a Bill, he does so, not as a minister, but as a member of the House to which he belongs. There is no difference in form between a Government Bill and a private member's Bill, between a Bill introduced by a member of the Government and a Bill introduced by any other member. But the chances of the Bill being passed into law are very different in the two cases. A private member's Bill has little chance of becoming law unless it relates to some comparatively unimportant or uncontroversial subject. When a private member undertakes legislation on his own account he finds himself handicapped in many ways. He has difficulty in obtaining expert assistance in the preparation o his Bill. He has difficulty in finding parliamentary time for its discussion. Even if the time is found, he has difficulty in commanding and organizing forces sufficient to overcome parliamentary opposition. Sir Alan Herbert, in *The Ayes have it,* has written a lively account of the adventures encountered by the private member's Bill which became the Matrimonial Causes Act, 1937. In surmounting all these obstacles the Government, as compared with the private member, enjoys great advantages. It has at its disposal a staff of experts for the preparation of Bills, and for the collecting and sifting of information on all points relating to the subject-matter of the Bill. It has also command of parliamentary time. Normally, during the earlier part of each session, Fridays are set apart for private members' Bills, and members who wish to introduce Bills draw lots for precedence on those Fridays. Unless a private member's Bill is so simple and uncontroversial as to meet with no opposition from any quarter, and so manages to slip through by consent, his only chance of getting it read a second time depends on his securing an early place on some Friday; and unless that Friday falls early in the session, the probability of the Bill making further progress is small. But the Government have at their disposal the greater part of the time available for parliamentary discussions, and can use all the machinery of party organization and party discipline for pushing their measures through. At the best, therefore, it could not be a matter for surprise that, although private members' Bills might largely outnumber Government bills, the proportion of them which became law was, by comparison, extremely small. Even this slender prospect of success vanishes in times of war or emergency when the private member must submit (as he may also have to do during the congested part of a session) to a Government monopoly of parliamentary time which gives him no chance at all.

It is on the Government, then, that by far the greatest share of responsibility for parliamentary legislation devolves; it is the Government that prepares, introduces, and steers through parliament all the more important legislative proposals which find their place as laws on the statute book. To say that at present the Cabinet legislates with the advice and consent of parliament would, as has been remarked by a distinguished American writer, hardly be an exaggeration. More and more the Prime Minister dictates the list of Bills and the programme of business, in conditions which show from day to day whether he does or does not enjoy the confidence of the majority. The private member often complains that his share in the work of legislation has been unduly curtailed. He may perhaps derive some consolation from the reflection that modern practice gives effect, though by different methods, to the old parliamentary formula of enactment. According to that formula it is the king who enacts laws with the advice and consent of parliament. According to modern practice it is the king's ministers who initiate and are mainly responsible for shaping all the more important measures of legislation. The ministry, who represent the executive Government, cannot, as such, decide whether a private member's Bill should or should not be introduced, or should or should not be passed, but they have, through their control over the business arrangements of the House of Commons, much to say as to the chances of any given measure becoming law. And though they cannot dictate the ultimate form which a Bill is to assume, they can by suggestion or persuasion, do much to determine that form.

The possible course of parliamentary legislation may be illustrated by taking some imaginary Government measure and tracing its progress from its earliest stage to its conclusion. Suppose that the Cabinet, at the beginning of a peace-time session, decide to introduce a comprehensive measure of local government reform, and to make it a leading feature in their legislative programme for the coming year. The first step will be to give instructions to the Government draftsman to prepare a Bill. There are seven Government draftsmen, bearing the official title of Parliamentary Counsel. They and their assistants are attached to the Treasury, as the central department of the Government; no other department can give them instructions without the authority of the Treasury. These instructions are usually very general in the first instance, and it is by means of personal conferences and discussions that the scheme of the Bill is gradually worked out. The measure may be referred to a committee of the Cabinet, who will assist the minister in charge of the Bill in considering questions of principle. The first crude sketch will be gradually elaborated. The draftsman will have daily conferences with the minister, or with the permanent head of the department concerned, or with both. There will be interviews and correspondence with experts in various branches of the subject with which the measure deals. Blue books and white papers may have to be mastered. Notes will be written tracing the history of previous legislation or attempted legislation, explaining the reasons for and effect of the several proposals embodied in the draft Bill, and these will soon grow into a formidable literature of commentaries. Thus the measure will probably have gone through a long period of gestation before its introduction into parliament.

Information and opinions on different points will have been confidentially obtained from various quarters; the provisions of the measure will have assumed many varying forms, and the alternatives will have been carefully discussed and compared. Yet, in spite of these precautions, as soon as the measure has been introduced, swarms of amendments will begin to settle down on the notice paper like clouds of mosquitoes. The minister in charge of the Bill has to scrutinize all these, with the help of his permanent staff and of the draftsman, to formulate reasons for their acceptance or rejection, and to prepare replies to, or amendments for meeting, the numerous points raised. Letters and articles appear in the newspapers. Questions are asked in the House.

Correspondence pours in from all parts of the country. The peculiar circumstances of the parish of Ockley-cum-Withypool must surely have been overlooked by the framers of the Bill. There will be Local Acts which require consideration. There may be vested interests. Journalists may write eloquent leaders, members of parliament may make sonorous speeches about the effect which the measure will have in promoting the welfare or undermining the institutions of the country. But to the parish beadle of Little Peddlington the question of supreme importance is how it will affect his emoluments, existing and prospective. It is with reference to them that he studies the parliamentary debates, indites missives to his representative, and organizes deputations to departments. Every member of parliament knows this beadle, under various names.

Questions of this kind occupy all the working time during the interval between the second reading and committee, and during the progress of the committee stage. Inside the House the minister is battling with amendments, some from enemies anxious to make the Bill unworkable or to reduce its operations to a minimum, others from indiscreet friends. Amendments are often framed hastily, without reference to grammar, logic, consistency, or intelligibility. They are apt to be crowded in at the beginning of each clause or sentence, with the view of obtaining precedence in discussion. The language of a law ought to be precise, accurate, and consistent, but the atmosphere of a crowded or heated assembly is not conducive to nicety or accuracy of expression. Decisions often have to be taken on the spur of the moment, and in view of the possibility of a snap division. At last the amendments are cleared off the paper; the new clauses, often raising the same questions, are disposed of; and the much-buffeted craft, with tattered sails, the deck encumbered with wreckage, and with several ugly leaks in her hold, labours heavily into a temporary harbour of refuge. There is a short interval for the necessary repairs, and then the struggle begins again at the 'report' stage. There may or may not be a sufficient opportunity for making such formal amendments as are necessary to make the measure decently consistent and intelligible. If not, they must be left for the House of Lords.

This is no unfair description of the methods of parliamentary legislation in normal conditions. It is therefore not surprising that both the methods and the results have been severely criticized. But the countervailing considerations have to be borne in mind.

Popular legislation has its defects, but it has its advantages also, and in the English view the advantages preponderate. It is true that the provisions of a Bill as introduced into parliament ought to be, and often are, perspicuous, consistent, orderly, and luminous, and that their perspicuity is often marred, the principle of their arrangement upset, their consistency disturbed, by amendments in committee. On the other hand, the substantial improvements which are effected often do more than atone for any deterioration in form.

The searching ordeal to which Bills are exposed in their passage through parliament frequently brings out defects and omissions against which the most skilful draftsman could not be expected to provide, which the most omniscient official could not be expected to foresee.

And the opportunities which the existing procedure and practice afford for the avoidance of ill-considered, ill-drawn, or inconsistent amendments, and for the removal of formal defects, are greater than are realized by those who are not familiar with parliamentary habits.

At first sight nothing would seem more preposterous than to submit a complicated draft for criticism and correction to a miscellaneous assembly of some 600 persons. But if the member in charge of a Bill is a minister with a compact and strong following at his back, and if he has the qualities which command the confidence and respect of the House, he can retain control over both the form and the substance of his Bill through all the vicissitudes of a discussion in committee.

It is true that the qualities required for the successful steering of a complicated and controversial Bill through committee are qualities of a very high order. They include tact, readiness, resourcefulness, firmness, and, above all, patience and good temper. The slightest appearance of dictation, the slightest loss of temper, will often set the House aflame. But if the minister can be conciliatory without 'wobbling', can distinguish between amendments which are fatal to his scheme and those which are not, can by a happy and timely suggestion indicate the way out of a confusing discussion, and can suppress his own impatience until it is shared by the committee, he can, without going to a division, often persuade his critics either to withdraw, or to modify, or to postpone their amendments, or at the worst, make his assent to their acceptance subject to further consideration at a later stage of the Bill.

Qualities of this kind are not rare amongst English statesmen, and are developed by parliamentary training. Those who have been in the habit of attending legislative discussions, whether in committee of the whole House or in any of the Standing Committees, cannot fail to have been struck by their display, and to have been also impressed by the good sense, good temper, and readiness to adopt compromises and accept reasonable assurances which characterize a committee, except when it has got 'out of hand'.

The 'report' stage of a Bill supplies an opportunity for setting right things which have gone wrong in committee, and amendments which cannot be made at the report stage can often be made in the House of Lords, which thus discharges to some extent the functions of a revising authority.

The foregoing description applies to Public Bill legislation, the legislation resulting in the Acts of Parliament which alter the general law of the country. Private Bill legislation is governed by different rules, and follows a different course of procedure.

The object of a Private Bill (which must, of course, be distinguished from a private member's Bill) is not to alter the general law of the country, but to alter the law relating to some particular locality or to confer rights on or relieve from liability some particular person or persons. When Private Bills become law they are classified as Local and Private Acts. They include measures for conferring further powers on particular local authorities, or for altering their constitution, and for similarly extending the powers of water, gas, and electricity companies, and the like.

The introduction of a Private Bill must be preceded by certain notices the object of which is to supply information to persons whose private interests are likely to be affected by the proposals of the Bill, such as persons whose land it is proposed to take for an undertaking which is to be authorized. In many cases plans and sections, showing the nature of the work proposed, and estimates of the expenditure proposed, have also to be deposited before particular dates and in particular places specified by the Standing Orders of the two Houses of Parliament. Detailed provision for all these matters is made by the Standing Orders, and there are officers (called Examiners), who are charged with the duty of seeing that the requirements of these Standing Orders have been complied with before a Private Bill is introduced into either House. If these requirements have been complied with, the Bill may be presented and read a first time and it is for the House to say, as in the case of a Public Bill, whether it shall be read a second time or not. As a rule the second reading of a Private Bill is not refused except on the ground that it raises some question of general principle which ought to be decided before the Bill is allowed to go further. If it is read a second time it is referred to a small committee, usually of four members. There is a slightly different and naturally swifter procedure for Bills which are unopposed. Every Private Bill has a preamble stating the reasons why recourse to this form of legislation is considered expedient, and the first business of the committee is to consider whether, in their opinion, the preamble is proved—in other words, whether there is a sufficient case for legislation. If they are satisfied on this point, they go through the clauses of the Bill, make such amendments as they think desirable, and report the Bill to the House. The proceedings of the committee are of a judicial nature, and, both on the preamble, and on the clauses and the proposed amendments, they hear the arguments of counsel, take evidence from witnesses, and consider reports from public departments. In fact their work, though in form legislative, would in many other countries be considered administrative, and would be dealt with, on administrative principles, by some department of the executive government.

When a Private Bill has been reported by a committee to the House, the report has to be considered by the House, and the Bill has to be read a third time and passed, as in the case of a Public Bill. But here again, as on second reading, opposition is rare except on some grounds of general principle. The practice and usage of each House of Parliament is to consider that the questions raised by Private Bills can be more satisfactorily settled by a small special committee than by a large assembly.

In two respects Private Bill procedure differs from what has already been said of Public Bills. In the first place a Private Bill begins by petition as Public Bills no longer do. The Standing Orders of the two Houses require the petition to be deposited by a fixed date in the year, though this requirement is relaxed in a proper case. In the second place, because Private Bills are expensive, it is usual to allow those which have not completed all their stages by the end of a session to be carried over into the next session, notwithstanding the general rule that a prorogation of Parliament, in terminating the session, wipes the parliamentary slate clean. This concession of 'carrying-over' facilities, which is not —though, if desired, it could be—allowed to Public Bills, means that the uncompleted Private Bill in effect begins afresh in the new session at the stage at which it left off. The expense of Private Bills is accounted for by such items as the House fees charged under the Standing

Orders of the two Houses, the cost of printing, the fees of parliamentary agents who act for promoters and opponents, and the fees, often substantial, of counsel practising at the parliamentary bar, who are not to be confused with the Parliamentary Counsel already mentioned as the official draftsmen of Public Bills. When Private Bills are unopposed, parliamentary agents conduct the proceedings and counsel are not heard.

The tendency of Private Bill legislation is to decrease in volume and importance. General Acts, such as the Public Health Act of 1875 and its successors, or the Water Act of 1945, have superseded many of the provisions which used to be inserted in special Acts; many things which used to require the authority of a special Act could later be effected by means of the much less expensive machinery of a 'provisional order' or a 'special order'. A provisional order is made by some department of the Government, such as the Ministry of Health, after the publication of local notices and the holding of a local inquiry; it will contain provisions of the same nature as those inserted in a Private Bill. When it has been made by the department it requires confirmation by parliament. For the purpose of obtaining this confirmation a minister representing the department concerned introduces a Bill confirming the order or a batch of orders, and this Bill goes through the same stages as an ordinary Private Bill. Of course it may be opposed, and if it is opposed at the committee stage much expense may be incurred. But as a rule the preliminary local inquiry suffices for the consideration and satisfaction of objections, and the great majority of Provisional Order Confirmation Bills pass through parliament without opposition.

A special order has a shorter and simpler career. A department lays the order in draft before parliament; the order takes effect as soon as both Houses have approved it by a resolution. Somewhere between the provisional and the special order is the type of order contemplated by the Statutory Orders (Special Procedure) Act of 1945—an experiment designed to be a cheaper and speedier substitute for a provisional order. A special procedure order, if unopposed, takes perhaps half the time needed for an unopposed provisional order.

It is not always easy to draw the line between Public and Private Bills, nor is it always easy to determine, as a matter of legislative discretion, in what cases it is expedient to allow Private Acts to make local modifications of the general law. Much useful general legislation has been preceded and facilitated by Acts which have enabled experiments to be tried locally. But it is obvious that legislation of this kind requires careful watching. Parliamentary committees, when they consider a Private Bill, do not lightly accept variations from precedent which may conflict with, deviate from, or exceed the provisions of the general law.

Hitherto we have been speaking of law made in the form of statutes, the direct legislation of parliament. We must not omit, however, to take note of the 'Statutory Instruments' (formerly called 'Statutory Rules and Orders') which are the children of statutes. This label covers all the officially published Orders in Council, administrative regulations, rules of court and other documents of a legislative character made by Government departments or other public bodies under the specific authority of some parent statute. Many Acts of Parliament delegate the legislative function, especially for meeting emergencies or for elaborating consequential technical or procedural detail. This delegation is not novel; the power, for instance, to make ministerial orders varying a statutory list of assize towns has a pedigree over five centuries old. Nor need the practice of delegation be accepted as proof of a naughty conspiracy by civil servants to acquire totalitarian authority. It has been developed because of its obvious convenience and flexibility and because Parliament could not otherwise enact the volume of legislation which the country is deemed to desire.

Conspicuous examples of 'crisis' law-making (like the Defence of the Realm Acts of 1914 and 1915 and the Emergency Powers (Defence) Act of 1939, or like the Emergency Powers Act of 1920, which can be brought into operation if the essentials of the life of the community are declared to be in danger) have authorized the making of codes of regulations prolific in a progeny of orders of all kinds, the grandchildren of the statute. Tiresome as these children and grandchildren may be, it will hardly be maintained that Parliament (which is not always in session) could deal satisfactorily with all these matters by direct legislation. Even a local attack of foot-and-mouth disease will not wait while a Bill is carried through all its stages in the two Houses of Parliament. It is hardly necessary to give examples of the other type of delegation, namely that which has for its purpose the working out of details, the prescribing of forms, or the framing of rules of procedure. The Factories Act authorizes the appropriate department to make regulations fixing, amongst other things, the standards of lighting, temperature, and ventilation in factories. Parliament has enacted the principle that there are to be standards; it has left it to the department to say what the standards shall from time to time be. If sometimes delegation seems to have been extended to cover points of principle as well as of detail, parliament has presumably had its reasons.

Naturally the exercise of these delegated powers cannot be left entirely uncontrolled. There will be a judicial check inasmuch as (except in the exceptional cases where parliament has expressly enacted the contrary) courts of law can declare the children or grandchildren of a statute to be invalid if they are *ultra vires*, i.e. outside the powers conferred by the parent Act. As for the parliamentary check, it has taken varying forms according to the particular conditions which the parent Act laid down. Save where the exercises of the delegated power are insignificant, it is usual for the Act to require them to be laid before parliament, so that, according to the particular conditions prescribed, the members of the two Houses can control this departmental or subordinate legislation either by confirming it by a resolution of approval or by taking advantage of a right to have it annulled on a resolution of disapproval. In some important cases, especially when the Statutory Instruments will be concerned with taxation or with the alteration of the text of a statute, the parent Act may require that the document be laid before parliament in draft, having no operative effect until confirmed by a resolution or address. The commonest formula of control allows the document to operate as soon as it is signed, but subjects it to the risk of being rejected and annulled if an adverse motion is successfully moved in either House within a time limit. These time limits, prescribed by the particular statute which authorized the department to legislate, were formerly far from uniform; in one instance the period was as long as 100 days, in another as short as 15. There was diversity also in the method of reckoning the days; the language of the statute did not always ensure that they should be days when parliament was continuously sitting. In 1946 the Statutory Instruments Act standardized the time limit, both for confirmation and rejection, at 40 days and standardized the reckoning so that periods when parliament is prorogued or dissolved, or when both Houses are adjourned for more than four days, are not counted.

It is unusual and indeed undesirable that parliament, having delegated the legislative power, should reserve to itself a right of amending the result. There is, for one thing, no suitable machinery for reconciling the consequences if the two Houses resolved upon different amendments.

Just as all members of parliament now take a more vigilant and a better instructed interest in the objects and clauses of a Bill than formerly, so also they are more alert to supervise departmental legislation. They feel that the output is so vast and so obtrusive in its impact upon the life of the people that there is a risk of some rule or order slipping through without receiving adequate attention. The House of Commons therefore set up in 1943 a Select Committee to scrutinize all the departmental legislation which may be the subject of proceedings in parliament, i.e. the rules, orders, or regulations which either require affirmative approval or are exposed to annulment on an adverse motion. This process of scrutiny is not intended to be concerned with the policy or merits of the document. A Select Committee cannot relieve the responsible minister of his responsibility to parliament. A report by the committee merely has the effect of waving a red light if something is detected of which parliament ought to take notice. A 'Special Orders Committee', set up by the House of Lords in 1925 to examine all departmental legislation which requires positive approval by a resolution of the House, has done valuable pioneer work in this direction.

The opportunities of approval or rejection do not, of course, exhaust the resources of parliamentary control. Parliament can at the outset refuse to allow departmental legislation to be substituted for direct law-making in the form of a statute; it can enact the revocation of regulations or orders which are objectionable; it can repeal the parent Act. These courses may not promise much success; the Government whips are likely to mobilize majorities in the division lobbies in favour of what the Government departments have done. But members of the House of Commons can, and do, make good use of the opportunities of question-time, the motion for the adjournment, or any other chance of exerting pressure.

Lastly, before leaving the field of delegated legislation, mention must be made of Church Assembly Measures. The Church of England Assembly (Powers) Act, 1919, sometimes called the Enabling Act, empowers the Church Assembly to pass Measures on any matter concerning the Church of England. The Measures are afterwards presented to parliament where they are examined by an Ecclesiastical Committee. If, after report from the committee, they obtain an affirmative resolution in each House, they are submitted, like a Bill which has completed all its stages, for the royal assent.

The rejection by the House of Commons of the resolution relating to the Prayer-book Measure in 1928 shows that parliament retains a real control, while it is relieved of the difficulty of direct legislation on a subject ill suited for party politics.

CHAPTER IV

FINANCE

THE EARLIEST function of parliament was to provide money for the use of the State, and this is still the most indispensable function of the House of Commons.

The general principles which govern the financial action of parliament had their classic exposition in the language, often quoted, of Sir Erskine May.

> 'The Crown, acting with the advice of its responsible ministers, being the executive power, is charged with the management of all the revenues of the country, and with all payments for the public service. The Crown therefore, in the first instance, makes known to the Commons the pecuniary necessities of the Government, and the Commons grant such aids and supplies as are required to satisfy these demands, and provide by taxes, and by the appropriation of other sources of the public income, the ways and means to meet the supplies which are granted to them. Thus the Crown demands money, the Commons grant it, and the Lords assent to the grant. But the Commons do not vote money unless it be required by the Crown; nor impose or augment taxes unless the taxation be necessary for the public service, as declared by the Crown through its constitutional advisers.'

These principles may be summed up in four leading rules. The first rule regulates the constitutional relations between the Crown and parliament in matters of finance. The Crown, that is to say the king, acting through his ministers who constitute the executive government, cannot raise money by taxation, borrowing or otherwise, or spend money, without the authority of parliament.

The second rule regulates the relations between the two Houses of Parliament. The power to grant money in parliament, a power which includes both the raising of money by tax or loan and the authorizing of expenditure, belongs exclusively to the House of Commons. The House of Lords assents to, and may (except as provided by the Parliament Act) reject, a grant of money, but cannot initiate or alter a grant.

The third rule imposes a restriction on the power of parliament to authorize expenditure. Parliament, that is to say the House of Commons, cannot vote money for any purpose whatsoever, except at the demand and upon the responsibility of ministers of the Crown.

The fourth rule imposes a similar restriction on the powers of taxation. Parliament, that is to say the House of Commons, cannot impose a tax, except upon the recommendation of the Crown. Accordingly any proposal for the levy of a new tax or for the increase of an existing tax must come from the Government. This rule applies only to general taxes, not to the taxes levied by local bodies for local purposes which are known as rates.

These rules are constitutional rules, based partly on Acts of Parliament such as the Bill of Rights and the Act of Settlement, and partly on parliamentary usage and practice. They have to be steadily borne in mind when the financial business of parliament is under consideration.

Such then are the main rules in accordance with which the House of Commons controls the raising and expenditure of the national revenue. That revenue is derived from several sources, but the chief source is taxation. The taxes imposed by the authority of parliament are partly permanent and partly temporary. Many of them are permanent, but, in order to maintain the control of parliament over the executive Government, some of the most important of them are imposed for a year only. Under the traditional practice the income tax, which is the most fruitful of the direct taxes, and the beer duty, which is one of the most important of the indirect taxes, have been renewed every year.

The whole of the national revenues, from whatever source derived, is, with some trifling exceptions, paid into the Bank of England or the Belfast branch of the Bank of Ireland, to the account of His Majesty's Exchequer, and is placed to the credit of a fund called the Consolidated Fund, and out of this fund all national payments are made. Thus there is, speaking broadly, one national till, into which all national receipts are paid and out of which all national payments are made.

That till is the Consolidated Fund, the creation of the younger Pitt, dating from 1787. Before that date the practice had been to charge the produce of specific taxes with the payments of specific debts, representing money borrowed by the State at different times for different purposes. There had been partial consolidations of these charges, but no general consolidation. What Pitt did by his great Act of 1787 was to carry practically all the national revenue of Great Britain, whether derived from taxes, Crown lands, or other sources, to one general account or fund called the Consolidated Fund, and to charge all the national debts on this fund. A similar measure was adopted for Ireland. For some years after the Union the debts of Great Britain and of Ireland were kept distinct, but in 1816 the Consolidated Funds of the two countries were united into the Consolidated Fund of the United Kingdom, which nowadays means Great Britain and Northern Ireland.

As there are two kinds of taxes, representing different degrees of control by parliament, so there are two classes of expenditure, one regulated by standing laws, the other by annual votes or appropriations. The public expenditure of the country is divided into two separate and distinct general heads, which are known in Treasury language as the Consolidated Fund charges and the Annual Supply charges. The first head includes the more permanent charges, which have been authorized by parliament to be paid from time to time when due, the Treasury being responsible for the time and mode of payment. The second head comprises the charges annually granted by parliament and thus brought under its immediate cognizance and control. Payments falling under the first head are described in statutory language as being made out of the Consolidated Fund. Payments under the second head are described as being made 'out of moneys provided by parliament'. The terminology is rather confusing to one not familiar with Treasury language and parliamentary procedure, because, as has been explained, all payments authorized by parliament, whether by permanent or by temporary appropriations, are made out of the Consolidated Fund. But the distinction is important, and materially affects the work of parliament.

The permanent charges include the annual charges for the national debt, for the civil list (that is to say, for the amounts granted at the beginning of each reign to defray the personal and household expenses of the king and queen and their family and the salaries of their personal staff), for the salaries of the judges, and for other payments of a fixed and permanent character.

Of these charges the first and most important is that for the national debt.

Into the history and various forms of the national debt it is impossible to enter here. It must suffice to say that what is called the funded debt, excluding terminable annuities, is debt on which the State is bound to pay interest at a fixed rate in the form of annuities, and the capital of which it is not bound to repay, but may repay at par, that is to say at the nominal value, on giving notice. Terminable annuities are merely a method by which a portion of this debt is paid off, by converting it into annuities charged at such a rate as to pay off principal and interest within a specified time. The unfunded debt consists of debt repayable within fixed periods and includes the floating debt, that is to say, Treasury bills, ways and means advances, and temporary borrowing from banks. Besides these forms of debt there are other forms of capital liabilities, such as the loans raised under special Acts for telegraph and telephone development, or for other purposes which parliament thinks may legitimately be met by borrowing.

Provision is made by law for the systematic reduction of the national debt in various ways, including what are called the old and the new sinking funds. These sinking funds have nothing to do with the sinking funds of the eighteenth century, when Pitt was persuaded for a time that debt might be extinguished by some magic operation of compound interest, though the fund for the purpose was itself raised by borrowing. It may be worth while to explain the nature of the modern sinking funds, as reference is frequently made to them in parliamentary debates on finance. It is a general rule that any grant made by parliament for the service of a particular financial year, i.e. the year ending 31 March, lapses so far as it is unexpended at the end of the year. The rule has often been criticized as tending to hasty and wasteful expenditure towards the close of the financial year. But it has the great advantage of enabling the national accounts to be made up and balanced, and the surplus or deficit ascertained, in each year, instead of letting the accounts run on unbalanced for an indefinite period. An Act of 1875 requires the Treasury to prepare within fifteen days after the expiration of every financial year an account of the public income and expenditure of the United Kingdom, showing the surplus of income or excess of expenditure during the year. If there be a deficit, it must be met in the following year by virtue of the Finance Act 1930. If there be a surplus of income, the surplus must be paid to the National Debt Commissioners, and applied by them towards purchasing, redeeming or paying off the national debt. This surplus is called the old sinking fund. It is sometimes made applicable, under special statutory provisions, in relief of the expenditure of a subsequent year, or toward some special expenditure, or, as in 1912, 1928, and 1929, carried to a suspense account. The same Act of 1875 imposed on the Consolidated Fund a permanent annual charge for the payment of interest on the national debt; any surplus not required for meeting the cost of interest and management was to be applied by the National Debt Commissioners towards the redemption of the debt. This surplus over the permanent annual charge was known as the new sinking fund. This 1875 provision has since been superseded. The Finance Act of 1928 established a fixed debt charge of £355,000,000. That 'permanent annual charge for the national debt' is to be issued during the year and applied in the first place to meet the cost of interest and management. The balance is the 'New Sinking Fund (1928)' and must be applied within nine months of its issue to meet the annual charges specified in the 1928 Act.

The observance of the rules, statutory and other, which regulate payments out of the Consolidated Fund is watched over by a permanent officer called the Comptroller and Auditor General. He holds office during good behaviour, subject to removal by the Crown on an address from the two Houses of Parliament. He cannot be a member of either House. His salary is fixed by statute and charged on the Consolidated Fund. He is an officer of the House, independent of the executive Government of the day. His double name indicates his dual functions. He controls the payments out of the Consolidated Fund by taking care that nothing is taken out without due authority. He subsequently audits the authorized expenditure, and satisfies himself that each payment was applied to the purpose to which it was appropriated.

We are now in a position to understand the steps which must be taken by the Government to obtain, with the co-operation of parliament, the necessary supplies for the year. The House of Commons has to do two things each year; first, to authorize the expenditure of such money as has to be provided by the annual votes, and secondly, to authorize the imposition of such taxes, other than permanent taxes, as may be required to meet the expenditure. The two operations go on concurrently, but the former begins first. The former culminates in the annual Appropriation Acts, the latter in the annual Finance Acts.

The first step is taken outside parliament, and consists in the preparation by the spending departments of estimates of their expenditure for the ensuing financial year. These are prepared towards the end of the calendar year, are submitted to and scrutinized by the Treasury, and are finally approved by the Cabinet.

It will be remembered that the House of Commons cannot vote money except in pursuance of a request or demand from the Crown. The demand for the money which has to be voted each year by the House of Commons is embodied in the King's Speech on opening parliament at the beginning of the session. The king, specially addressing the House of Commons, demands the annual supply for the public service, and acquaints the Commons that estimates will be laid before them of the amount that will be required. These estimates are presented to the House by the Government as soon as practicable afterwards. They are not submitted to the House of Lords, for that body has no concern with them.

In time of war it is neither easy to foresee the country's expenditure nor, for reasons of security, prudent to publish specific items. It is therefore found advisable to proceed by votes of credit in good round figures rather than by an exact system of estimates and appropriation. In normal times the ordinary annual estimates for the coming financial year are presented in four parts, each comprising one of the branches of the public service, namely, the navy, the army, the air force and the civil services. Each estimate contains, first, an estimate of the total grant thereby demanded, and then a statement of the detailed expenditure under each grant, divided into subheads or items.

At the beginning of each session, as soon as the address in reply to the King's Speech has been agreed to, the House of Commons sets up two committees, the Committee of Supply and the Committee of Ways and Means. These are committees of the whole House. They are not committees in the ordinary sense of the word, nor smaller bodies to which the House refers some matter for inquiry or consideration and report, or delegates some function, but merely, as explained in a previous chapter, the House itself transacting its business in a less formal manner, with the Speaker's chair vacant, and under the presidency of a chairman who sits at the table. The business of the Committee of Supply is to consider the estimates, and to vote such grants of money as appear to be required. The Committee of Ways and Means has two functions. It has to pass resolutions authorizing the imposition of any taxes which may be required. And it has to pass resolutions authorizing the issue out of the Consolidated Fund of the sums required to meet the grants voted by the Committee of Supply. The first of these functions is important, and will be considered in connexion with the budget. The other function is merely formal and consequential, and amounts to little more than authorizing cheques to be drawn for the expenditure already agreed to.

The Committees of Supply and Ways and Means are met with in the reign of Charles I. At that time supply and ways and means went more closely hand in hand than they do at present. The House would consider, in one committee, how much it would grant the king for some particular need, and, immediately afterwards, in another committee, what means it would adopt for raising the money required. At the present day the estimates give, at the beginning of the session, a comprehensive survey of the needs of the year, and later in the session the Chancellor of the Exchequer, by his budget statement, gives a comprehensive survey of the mode in which he proposes to meet these needs. But the old system has left its traces in the existing procedure.

The sittings of the Committee of Supply continue during the greater part of the session, and, under the existing Standing Orders, at least twenty days must be set apart for this purpose before the fifth of August in each year. But the business at these sittings is critical rather than financial, and will be dealt with as such in a later chapter. As a consequence of the principle that money cannot be voted except on the request of the Crown, the Committee of Supply cannot increase a grant asked for by the estimates. Nor can the Committee alter the destination of a grant. What the Committee does is to criticize the administration of money voted. Any such criticism must, in order to comply with the rules of the House, be based on a motion to reduce or reject a head or item in the estimates. But the rea object of this motion is usually to elicit an explanation of the proposed expenditure, or to ventilate some grievance connected with it, and, if the answer is at all satisfactory, the motion is usually dropped. As a rule the estimates are passed as they are presented.

The exigencies of the public service make it necessary to grant money before the criticism of its administration is completed. Before the end of the financial year, i.e. before the end of March, the government must have enough money in hand to carry on with during at least a portion of the next financial year. The navy, army, and air force are allowed to apply temporarily the surplus on any of their votes to some other navy, army, or air force purpose, and therefore in their case it is sufficient to take two or three big votes before the end of March. In the case of the civil services no similar transfer of funds is allowed, and therefore it is necessary for their purposes to take a vote on account sufficient to cover any period which may be considered desirable. The remaining navy, army, and air force votes, and, so far as they are not met by a vote on account, the civil service votes, are discussed on the days set apart for the Committee of Supply during the remainder of the session, and any votes which have not been previously considered and disposed of are passed *en bloc* on the last day on which the Committee sits. Besides the ordinary estimates for the year, it is often necessary to present estimates for supplementary or additional grants when the amount named in the ordinary estimate for a particular service is found to be insufficient for the purposes of the current year, or when a need arises during the current year for expenditure on some new service not contemplated in the ordinary estimates for that year.

In order to complete the steps required by law for the issue of public money, the resolutions passed by the Committee of Supply have to be reported to and confirmed by the House, sitting formally with the Speaker in the chair: supplemented by the necessary resolution in the Committee of Ways and Means, which has also to be reported and confirmed: and then finally confirmed by an Act of Parliament. One such Act, called a Consolidated Fund Act, has to be passed before the end of March, and similar Acts may become necessary during the course of the session. These Acts anticipate the final sanction given towards the end of the session by the annual Appropriation Acts. When the Committee of Supply has completed its work by passing all the votes asked for, and its resolutions have been supplemented by the consequential resolution in Committee of Ways and Means, and when all these resolutions have been agreed to by the House, the Bill which is to become the Appropriation Act for the year is brought in. The several votes passed by the Committee of Supply and confirmed by the House are scheduled to this Act, and the Act requires each grant so voted to be expended upon the service to which it is thereby appropriated.

It has been seen that the Comptroller and Auditor General is the officer responsible for seeing that the requirements of the law as to the issue of public money are duly observed. This is one of his functions. The other is to see that money issued is not applied to any purpose other than that to which it is appropriated. In order to do this he examines the accounts of the spending departments for each financial year, and then presents to the House of Commons what are known as the Appropriation Accounts, which cover in great detail the actual expenditure in all the services for which money is voted by the Committee of Supply, with his reports and comments thereon. This business of examination and report occupies much time, and the Appropriation Accounts for the year ending with the thirty-first of March in one year are usually presented in the February of the following year. They are then referred to a committee which is appointed for each session by the House of Commons, and is called the Committee of Public

Accounts. This Committee inspects the accounts, considers the reasons given for spending on each item more or less than the amount estimated, inquires into the items which need further expenditure, examining for this purpose the accounting officers of the departments and other persons, and makes a series of reports to the House.

Although the Public Accounts Committee could thus help the House of Commons to supervise the Appropriation Accounts, there was from time to time a demand for some further control of public expenditure and, in particular, some better review of the estimates than was possible in a committee of the whole House. Wars, because they involve heavy spending, have reinforced the demand. During the Crimean War and the South African War select committees were set up to examine such specific matters as the condition of the army before Sebastopol or the allegations of irregularity in War Office contracts. In 1902 a Select Committee on National Expenditure was appointed. Reappointed next year, it recommended the constitution of an Estimates Committee which would dovetail its work with that of the Public Accounts Committee. Under growing pressure such a committee was at length created in 1912, but it came to an end on the outbreak of war in 1914. It had encountered the inherent difficulty of considering administration apart from policy ; ministers who must answer to Parliament for their departments cannot share with a committee the responsibility for estimates or for the policy behind the estimates. A fresh effort to review current expenditure was made in 1917 when another Select Committee on National Expenditure was set up. This body, reappointed in the next four sessions, usefully drew attention to the inadequate and baffling form of estimates and Appropriation Accounts, and, as the task of survey seemed too heavy for a single unit, recommended the sessional appointment of two or, if necessary, three standing committees on estimates. They also suggested that these committees should be assisted by a special officer of the House as 'Examiner of Estimates', but the House rejected this proposal. When this National Expenditure Committee came to an end in 1921, the Estimates Committee was revived in its place with a power (seldom used) to appoint sub-committees, and with the part-time help of a Treasury official. In December 1939 the National Expenditure Committee was once more constituted. Its task was

'to examine the current expenditure . . . for the defence services, for civil defence and for other services directly connected with the war, and to report what, if any, economies consistent with the execution of the policy decided by the Government, may be effected therein.'

Making good use of its power to appoint sub-committees, it developed in its members a specialized knowledge of particular departments' operations—a point worth noting because the normal select committee is less a collection of specialists than a microcosm of the House as a whole. The energy of this National Expenditure Committee was attested by the fact that, after five years' work, it (and its sub-committees) had held nearly 1,700 meetings, including visits to Government establishments and private undertakings, and had examined over 3,500 witnesses. Like its predecessor in 1918, however, it had to complain of the form in which estimates and accounts are presented to the House. Its reports make valuable material for considering the machinery of parliamentary control of finance. It is clear that, if liaison can be maintained between a Public Accounts Committee and an Estimates Committee, there is fine work to be done under a strong chairman by members who can spare the time. The story shows that financial scrutiny cannot be attempted so hopefully by the great mass of members in committee of the whole House as by select committees whose proceedings, in the words of the National Expenditure Committee of 1903,

> are usually devoid of party feeling, who may obtain, accurate knowledge collected for them by trained officials which may, if desired, be checked or extended by the examination of witnesses or the production of documents.'

Like the reports of the Comptroller and Auditor General, the reports of these committees have great value in checking laxity of administration. Extravagance they cannot stop: for this the Government and the House of Commons are responsible; but over irregularity of expenditure they exercise a potent control. Days are sometimes set apart for a discussion of these reports by the House, but it has usually been found difficult to induce the House to take much interest in the financial irregularities of past years.

So much for the control exercised by the House of Commons over expenditure. What remains to be considered is the control of the House over taxation.

Once in every year, usually soon after Easter, the Chancellor of the Exchequer makes his budget statement in the Committee of Ways and Means. He reviews the finance of the past year, comparing estimated with actual results, and then estimates his requirements for the current or forthcoming year, and explains the mode in which he proposes to raise revenue for meeting them. In so doing he always tries to make as close an approximation as possible between estimated revenue and estimated expenditure. If the estimated revenue on the existing basis is more than sufficient to meet estimated expenditure, he may be in a position to remit or reduce taxes. If it is insufficient, he may have to increase existing taxes or impose new taxes. His proposals are embodied in resolutions which are usually handed in at the table of the House immediately after the conclusion of his budget statement, and one at least of them is usually passed on the same night. The budget resolutions, like the resolutions of the Committee of Supply, do not obtain complete legal effect until they have been confirmed by an Act of Parliament. But it is necessary to prevent the lapse of such annual taxes as it is intended to continue, and also to guard against the loss of revenue which would in many cases arise if there were an interval between the announcement of intention to increase or impose a tax and the date at which the increase or imposition takes effect. If, in normal times, the intention to increase the duty on tea were announced before the date at which the increased duty took effect, tea would instantly pour into the ports at the lower rate. Consequently, under an Act passed in 1913, modifying a practice which had dated back at least to the time of Blackstone in the eighteenth century, a resolution for the imposition of a tax which ought on fiscal grounds to come into operation immediately takes provisional effect at once. If the resolution is approved by parliament it is embodied in and confirmed by an Act of Parliament, which for that purpose has a retrospective effect. If it should be modified in its passage through the House of Commons, any amount collected in excess of that ultimately authorized would be refunded.

The budget resolutions proposed by the Chancellor of the Exchequer are discussed in the Committee of Ways and Means, which can reject or amend any resolution, but cannot, except at the instance of a minister of the Crown, increase the amount proposed to be raised by taxes. When the resolutions have been passed by the Committee and agreed to by the House, they form the foundation of a Bill which goes through the same stages as other Bills, and which, when it becomes law, is known as the Finance Act.

Formerly it was the practice to have several taxing Acts for each year. Different taxes or sets of taxes, and proposals relating to revenue administration and the national debt, were dealt with by different measures. It was in pursuance of this practice that Gladstone's proposal in 1860 to repeal the paper duties was embodied in a separate Bill. But the rejection of this Bill by the House of Lords led to an alteration of practice. The Lords had always asserted the right to reject money Bills, but had never ventured to amend them. In order to make the exercise of this right of rejection more difficult, Gladstone in 1861 brought in a comprehensive taxing Bill, dealing with all the taxes which were to be imposed or continued, and including a repeal of the paper duties. The practice thus established has ever since been continued, and has been developed. Until 1894 the taxing Act of the year was known as the Customs and Inland Revenue Act. In that year its title was changed to the Finance Act, a title which it has ever since retained. Under that title it usually includes, not only all the taxes imposed or continued for the financial year, but such fiscal regulations as may be required in relation either to the revenue or to the national debt. But some of these regulations are occasionally embodied in a separate supplemental measure such as the Income Tax (Employments) Act, which introduced the 'pay as you earn' system in 1943.

Taxation is not the only way in which money is raised for the needs of the State. As in the case of all other business concerns, it is also necessary to borrow, either in anticipation of the ordinary receipts of the year, or to meet expenditure which cannot reasonably be expected to be defrayed out of the income of the year. Every Consolidated Fund Act and every Appropriation Act contains a provision empowering the Treasury to borrow money by short loans in the form of Treasury bills, or otherwise, to the extent of the expenditure authorized by the Act. Loans of this kind form the great mass of the floating debt, and it was by the help of such loans that the Government was able to carry on its work for some time after the rejection of the Finance Bill in 1909. Loans for longer periods require special legislation, which has to be preceded by resolutions similar to those which precede an ordinary Finance Bill.

If we ask how far the control of the House of Commons over expenditure and taxation is effective, the answer will probably be that over irregularity of expenditure the system of control is, on the whole, effective and satisfactory, that over amount of expenditure the control is not very effective, but that the control over taxation is substantial.

When a Government is charged with extravagance,

the reply is usually made, and is made with truth, that the pressure of the House of Commons is in the direction of expenditure rather than of economy. Economy is preached in the abstract, but the demands for expenditure are more specific and detailed, more persistent, and therefore more effective. Nothing is more difficult or more unpopular than administrative economy. Attempts in this direction have to encounter, not only arguments based on efficiency, but the still more formidable opposition proceeding from the numerous private and personal interests which would be adversely affected by retrenchment. The real custodian of the public purse, the watchdog against claimants on public funds, is the Treasury, and the Treasury is not popular.

To tax and to please, said Burke, is not given to men, any more than to love and to be wise. Any proposals for taxation which the Chancellor of the Exchequer may bring forward are pretty sure to be met by vigilant and well-informed criticism and to encounter formidable opposition.

It is true that he can exercise greater control over the fortunes of his budget than the finance ministers of many other countries. In pre-1939 France the budget proposals were referred to a very strong budget committee, which took them completely out of the hands of the finance minister, and often returned them in a shape quite inconsistent with his general financial scheme. In Germany the position was much the same. But in Britain the Chancellor of the Exchequer retains his conduct of, and responsibility for, his financial resolutions, and the Bill founded on them, from the beginning to the end of their parliamentary career. He has, of course, to fight them through the House as best he can, and meet the criticisms which assail him from every quarter; consequently his proposals often undergo substantial transformation before they emerge in the form of law.

CHAPTER V

ADMINISTRATION

PARLIAMENT DOES not govern. Parliamentary government does not mean government by parliament. Once, and once only, in the course of English history has the House of Commons attempted to administer the affairs of the country through executive committees, and the precedent set by the Long Parliament has not been followed.

What is done by parliament, and especially by the House of Commons, is in the first place to secure that the king's ministers, who control and are responsible for the executive government of the country, shall represent and have the confidence of the party (or combination of parties) which commands a majority in the House, and in the next place to control the action of those ministers by means of questions and criticisms.

Any member has the right to address a question to any minister of the Crown, being also a member of the House, about the public affairs with which he is officially connected, or about a matter of administration for which he is responsible. The proper object of such a question is to obtain information on a matter of fact within the special cognizance of the minister, and the rules and practice of the House limit the right to ask questions so as to confine them to this object. The practice of putting questions to ministers developed rapidly during the latter half of the nineteenth century and tended to occupy so much time that restrictions became necessary. A member must not ask more than three questions a day. Naturally the minister must have time to prepare his answer. If a member wishes his question to be answered orally, he marks it with an asterisk and, under a sessional order introduced in 1946, he must give at least two days' notice of it. A written answer is expected within seven days. A period of about three-quarters of an hour is set apart on sitting days other than Fridays for the answering of such questions. During that period supplementary questions may be asked within limits determined by the Speaker, but no debate is allowed to arise, and in this respect the English practice differs from the 'interpellations' of the French chamber. A minister cannot be compelled to answer a question, and sometimes declines to do so on the ground of public interest. It is for him to determine what kind of answer is likely to be considered proper and sufficient in the circumstances of the case. An unsatisfactory answer may give rise to a debate on the motion for adjournment of the House at the end of business. But such a motion is not allowed unless the matter to be discussed is a 'definite matter of urgent public importance', and the Speaker is strict in his interpretation of this rule. The answers to 'unstarred' questions, and to 'starred' questions for which time cannot be found within the allowed period, are printed in Hansard and circulated to members subsequently.

Asking questions in the House is one of the easiest methods by which a member can notify to his constituents the attention which he devotes to public affairs and to their special interests. For this and other reasons, the right to ask questions is specially liable to abuse, and its exercise needs careful supervision by the Speaker and those acting under his authority. But there is no more valuable safeguard against maladministration, no more effective method of bringing the searchlight of criticism to bear on the action or inaction of responsible ministers and their subordinates. A minister has to be constantly asking himself, not merely whether his proceedings and the proceedings of those for whom he is responsible are legally or technically defensible, but what kind of answer he can give if questioned about them in the House and how that answer will be received.

The asking of questions is not the only mode in which the House can obtain information from or through the Government. It can, on the motion of any member, obtain returns supplying such information on matters of public importance as is obtainable through departments of the Government. A motion for a return, unless unopposed, has little chance while the Government monopolizes members' time. It may be opposed on grounds of public policy, such as that the disclosure of the information sought is not for the public interest, or that its supply would involve unreasonable labour and expense. The Government can also, and frequently does, on its own initiative, lay papers before the House, papers technically known as 'command papers' because they are supposed to be presented by command of the king, or more popularly described in general terms as 'white papers'. Other methods of obtaining information are the appointment of a parliamentary committee, of a royal commission, or of a departmental committee, and these methods are often adopted, at the instance of parliament, when the object is to collect, consider, and formulate suggestions for legislative or administrative reforms. A parliamentary committee is appointed and constituted by an order of the House, and is armed by the House with the power of requiring the attendance of witnesses and the production of papers. It cannot sit except when the House is sitting. It is appointed for one session only, so that if its work is left unfinished at the end of the session, it must be reappointed. Sometimes there is a joint committee of the two Houses, consisting of members selected by and from each House. When the questions to be discussed raise political issues a parliamentary committee is usually preferred to a royal commission or departmental committee. A royal commission is appointed and constituted by the king on a submission by the Prime Minister; the Home Secretary submits the warrant and counter-signs it. It has no power to compel the attendance of witnesses or the production of documents unless this power is conferred on it by a special Act of Parliament. On the other hand, its sittings and duration are independent of the sittings of parliament. A departmental committee is appointed and constituted by a minister of the Crown to inquire into and report on some matter connected with the business of his department. Its functions and powers are much the same as those of a royal commission. Under an Act of 1921 His Majesty or a Secretary of State may appoint a tribunal for inquiring into any matter of urgent public importance if both Houses of Parliament so resolve. This procedure, adopted for instance for the budget disclosure inquiry in 1936, gives the tribunal the powers of the High Court as regards witnesses and documents.

The papers laid before either House of Parliament, under an order of the House, or on the initiative of a minister, the returns periodically presented in pursuance of directions in Acts of Parliament, and the reports of committees and commissions, make up the formidable mass of official papers popularly known as 'blue books'.

Questions and motions for returns are means for obtaining information on which criticism may be based, but do not themselves supply opportunities for criticism. Such opportunities are afforded in various ways.

At the beginning of each session amendments may be framed on the address in reply to the King's Speech in such a way as to raise a debate on almost any question of general policy or public administration. The questions usually selected are those which at the moment excite most general interest, and the debate on them may extend over several days.

Any member is entitled to bring forward a motion condemning or criticizing the Government or any member or department of the Government. If such a motion were made by the leader of the opposition, it would be treated as a vote of want of confidence, and time would be given by the Government for its discussion. But the opportunities afforded to other members for the exercise of this right are, in practice, severely limited. Normally in the early part of the session a certain number of evenings, at first two in each week, afterwards one, have been set apart for private members' motions, members being allowed to ballot for priority on these evenings. But these evenings have often been taken by the Government under pressure of business; they have tended to disappear altogether after Whitsuntide, and, while available, have not always been utilized to the best advantage. As we shall see in our next chapter, an experiment initiated during the Second World War compensated the private member for the eclipse of his rights by giving him the opportunity of nightly debates on the adjournment when he can ventilate a grievance or voice his criticism of the administration. He always had this remedy, provided that time permitted; but now he is assured of it however late the hour.

More frequent and regular opportunities for reviewing and criticizing the action of the Government are afforded by the various steps which, as previously explained, must be taken to obtain supply, that is, to authorize expenditure. From the old constitutional principle, asserted in the earliest parliaments, that the redress of grievances should precede the grant of supply, it has been deduced as a parliamentary rule that the action of each minister, and of the departments and officers over whom he has control, can be discussed on the vote for the branch of expenditure concerned. On the motion for first going into Committee of Supply on the navy estimates, any question relating to the administration of the navy may be raised and discussed, and the same rule applies to the army and air force estimates and the civil service estimates. In the committee the discussion is confined to the particular vote or votes set down for consideration, though a wider range has been allowed to the debate on the first vote both in the navy estimates and in the army and air force estimates.

A minimum number of days, not less than twenty in each session before the 5th of August, must be allotted for these discussions. The votes to be taken on each of these days are fixed by arrangement between the party whips and are practically selected by the opposition as the natural and normal critic of the Government, subject to the reservation of two or three days for the discussion of grievances from Scotland and Northern

Ireland. Further opportunities for discussing administration, nominally in connexion with expenditure, are given by supplementary estimates, by votes on account, by the debates which may take place when votes in committee are reported to the House, and by the second and third reading stages of any Consolidated Fund Bill or Appropriation Bill, for at these stages the conduct or actions of any of those who receive or administer grants specified in and sanctioned by the Bill may be discussed. In this way, under the guise of fiscal discussion, every department of the government, every branch of the central administration, may have to run the gauntlet of parliamentary criticism. Other opportunities are offered by the motion for adjournment, particularly on the last day before a recess, when a wide range of subjects is discussed.

We sometimes hear about the tyranny exercised by Cabinets, and by the majority on whose support they depend. It is true that the executive government of the country takes a greater share in the initiation of legislative and financial proposals, and exercises greater control over their course through the legislature, than in many countries enjoying parliamentary institutions. It is also true that the bonds of party discipline tend to tighten. But the Government has to defend by argument all its legislative and financial proposals, and may be required to explain and justify any branch of its administrative action. It may be that the time allotted to the criticism of administration in Committee of Supply has too often been monopolized by bores or frittered away in the ventilation of unimportant grievances. The system has its defects, but it exercises a wholesome influence on the official world, and frequently gives rise to debates of great value and importance. Nothing clears the air more effectually than a good parliamentary debate, or reveals more distinctly the currents of popular feeling and public opinion, and the force with which they flow. Of the results of such a debate the division list is a very imperfect and fallacious test. The arguments and attitude of minorities and of individual members are potent in determining the action of the government.

It must be repeated that parliament does not govern, and is not intended to govern. A strong executive government, tempered and controlled by constant, vigilant, and representative criticism, is the ideal at which parliamentary institutions aim.

CHAPTER VI

SITTINGS AND PROCEDURE

Ever since the beginning of parliamentary history Westminster has been the place at which parliaments have been ordinarily held. They have been held elsewhere in exceptional circumstances, but Westminster has always been their normal home. The last occasion on which parliament sat outside London was the Oxford parliament of Charles II. The habits of Plantagenet kings were migratory, and, for reasons of war, state, or economy, they often shifted their quarters. But the Palace of Westminster, outside, yet conveniently near, their chief city, was their principal residence, and it was natural that the assemblies which developed into parliaments should usually be summoned to meet in their Westminster palace.

The old palace and the Abbey closely adjoined each other, and were practically contiguous, for one passed into the Abbey through a gateway from Old Palace Yard, which was the inner court of the Palace. Which particular hall or room in the Palace was most frequently used for the meeting of the earliest parliaments is uncertain, but it is known that for many centuries, and down to the end of the eighteenth century, the Lords sat in an ancient building at its south end. This was the building which Guy Fawkes tried to blow up.

Whether in the earliest parliaments the two Houses sat together, and if so at what time they began to sit apart, is also still a matter of discussion among historians.

Perhaps one is entitled to ask whether it is certain that they sat at all. As has been remarked in an earlier chapter, the proceedings of these parliaments resembled those of an eastern durbar, and one may picture to oneself the king sitting on his throne, with seats for some of his great nobles and prelates, but with no more than standing room for the majority of the assembly. These would group themselves as dignity and convenience suggested, the barons who represented themselves often mingling with the knights of shires who represented counties, and separated by no physical barrier from the citizens and burgesses. However this may have been, we know that early in the reign of Edward III the Commons were, after the opening of parliament, directed to withdraw for their deliberations into a separate chamber. Their place of deliberation seems to have been usually in the adjoining Abbey, either the Chapter-house or the Refectory. Direct evidence on the subject is scanty and imperfect, but tradition is uniform that until the end of Henry VIII's reign their usual place of sitting was the Westminster Chapter-house. It was conveniently near the Palace, and we may surmise that its use for this secular purpose was as much by order of the king as by permission of the abbot. The relations between Palace and Abbey, king and abbot, were very close, and it did not suit either to examine too minutely the authority of the other. Plantagenet kings kept their treasure in the Abbey, close to the Chapter-house, and exercised rights over this part of the building. And to this day the Chapter-house is, as the presence of policemen indicates, under the custody, not of the dean, but of the king's chief Commissioner of Works who is now, after many recent changes of title, the Minister of Works.

Henry VIII disestablished and disendowed the foundation of St. Stephen's Chapel, which had been the royal chapel of the Palace, and in 1547, the first year of his successor's reign, this chapel was set apart for the use of the House of Commons, and continued to be its home until the fire of 1834. After demolitions and alterations which began in 1800, the Lords sat in a large hall known at various times as the White Hall and the Court of Requests, on a line with Westminster Hall, and situated where the statue of Richard Cœur de Lion now stands. At right angles to this hall, and therefore parallel to St. Stephen's Chapel, was an old building called the Painted Chamber, from the decorations on its walls. In this chamber conferences between the two Houses were usually held. The fire of 1834 destroyed the whole of the ancient palace, except Westminster Hall and except the crypt and part of the cloisters of St. Stephen's Chapel. But the hall then used as the House of Lords, and the Painted Chamber, were temporarily repaired and fitted up, the first for the Commons, the second for the Lords.

The new palace which rose on the ruins of the old was designed by Sir Charles Barry, and took many years to construct. The Lords first occupied their new quarters on 13 April 1847, the Commons theirs on 13 May 1850.

The old palace had ceased to be a royal residence after a destructive fire early in Henry VIII's reign, but it remained a royal palace. Its successor is still a royal palace, and, as such, is under the charge of the Lord Great Chamberlain, an hereditary officer of state.

The rooms set apart in the palace for the sittings of the two Houses faced each other in such a way that, through the intervening hall and corridors, the king's throne at the south end of the House of Lords would, if all intervening doors were open, be visible from the Speaker's chair at the north end of the House of Commons. At right angles to them and to Westminster Hall is St. Stephen's Hall, lined by statues of parliamentary statesmen, and occupying the site of St. Stephen's Chapel. This was the home of the House of Commons for nearly 300 years. They were to reassemble there, as we shall see, on a memorable day in 1945.

The chamber in which the House of Commons sat from 1850 onwards was constructed on the same general lines as the old chapel of St. Stephen, and like it, did not provide sitting accommodation for anything like the total number of members. In the body of the House there were less than 350 seats for more than 600 members. But, for discomfort in crowding, there was compensation in ease of hearing. Anyone could make himself heard without straining his voice, and business debates were therefore far more practicable than in the spacious chamber allotted to the House of Representatives at Washington. The accident that the House of Commons sat in a narrow room, with benches facing each other and not with seats arranged like those of a theatre, made for the two-party system and against groups shading into each other. In the House of Lords there were cross benches, but there were none in the House of Commons.

This traditional arrangement of opposed benches the Commons decided to perpetuate when the destruction of their chamber by enemy action in 1941 gave them the chance to vary its future plan. Mr. Winston Churchill persuasively advocated the reproduction of the old House with its intimate conditions of debate and the sense of crowd and urgency and excitement upon great occasions.

'We shape our buildings [he said], and afterwards our buildings shape us . . . Logic is a poor guide compared with custom; logic has created in many countries semi-circular assemblies with buildings which give every member not only a seat to sit in but often a desk to write at and a lid to bang. . . . The essence of good House of Commons speaking is the conversational style, the facility for quick informal interruption and interchange; haranguing from a rostrum would be a bad substitute.'

These sentiments prevailed and the task of rebuilding on the old lines was begun in 1945.

Barry's building had offered a vulnerable target. Long before a high-explosive bomb did the first serious damage near St. Stephen's Porch in the autumn of 1940, forethought had prepared for the removal of parliament to a secret destination (revealed, when the war was over, as Stratford-on-Avon), if need should arise. The scheme, however, was soon repudiated; members were eager to share what others suffered.

'As to evacuation [said Mr. Churchill], everyone must remain at his post and discharge his daily duty. This House would be affronted if any suggestion were made to it that it should change its location from London. Here we began the war and here will we see it ended.'

Prudence dictated, nevertheless, that some alternative site should be prospectively available. Such a site (referred to as 'the Annexe' in the endeavour to keep secret what hundreds knew) was found near at hand on the west side of the Abbey at Church House, the home of the Church Assembly and the administrative headquarters of the Church of England. Here, in a modern structure already severely damaged by a heavy bomb which had wrecked the chief assembly-hall, parliament sat from time to time. Here the King opened a new session of parliament in 1940. Here the House sat in the following May after the Commons chamber had been destroyed. Five weeks after that catastrophe, however, Lords and Commons were back in the Palace of Westminster, the Lords having generously placed their own chamber at the disposal of the Commons and finding for themselves less spacious accommodation in the King's Robing Room. The flying bombs caused another temporary migration to Church House in 1944, though members at all times preferred the accustomed amenities of Barry's building. During the rocket bomb attacks sittings continued to be held in the Palace of Westminster. It was from that ancient meeting-place that the two Houses crossed the road in procession, the peers to Westminster Abbey, the Commons to their parish church of St. Margaret's, to give thanks when the war in Europe was won. When the Lords reoccupied their old home for the ceremonial opening of the new Parliament on 15 August 1945, the Commons, with a proper sense of the continuity of history, assembled on the site of St. Stephen's Chapel to await Black Rod's summons to attend His Majesty and hear the speech from the throne. They had last sat there on 15 August one hundred and eleven years before. And now, on the same day, the members of the two Houses crossed the road once more to a service of thanksgiving for the final victory.

So much must suffice for the place of sitting. In dealing with the time of sittings we must in the first place distinguish between a parliament, a session, and a sitting.

A new parliament is called together by means of writs of summons, which are sent out from the Crown Office, in pursuance of a proclamation and Order in Council. These royal directions summon peers, require the election of members of the House of Commons, and fix the day on which the parliament is to meet. The same proclamation dissolves one parliament and summons its successor; a general election intervenes between the death of the one and the birth of the other. It is the king, acting on the advice of his ministers, who determines the dates of dissolution and of meeting again. By the Septennial Act, as we have seen earlier, the duration of a parliament was limited to seven years; it was subsequently reduced by the Parliament Act to five years. Parliament can prolong its own life by altering the law, as it did annually from 1940 to 1944. On the other hand dissolution has often anticipated the running out of the full time.

Under the Plantagenet kings a few days often sufficed for the work of each parliament. In Tudor times parliaments lasted longer, and the practice grew up of having several distinct sessions of the same parliament. A session is terminated by prorogation, which, like dissolution, is effected by order of the king, acting on the advice of his ministers. Prorogation does not affect the seats of members, but puts an end to the current business of the session, and kills all Bills which have not become law before parliament is prorogued.

A sitting of either House is terminated by adjournment, and an adjournment, unlike a dissolution or prorogation, is the act of each House, independently of, and at different times from, the other House. It merely suspends the transaction of current business.

It is in the exercise of this power that each House adjourns its sittings from day to day and over the recesses which usually take place at Christmas, Easter, and Whitsuntide, and sometimes for a longer period in the autumn.

The opening of a new parliament, and of each new session, is attended by ceremonies which recall, and which date from, Plantagenet times. The king sits on his throne, with his great Officers of State before him. The benches of the House of Lords are occupied by the lords spiritual and temporal, clad in their robes, and by the peeresses. The judges, summoned as attendants, sit on their woolsacks, in the middle. The members of the Commons House find such room as they can, at or near the bar, with their Speaker at their head.

The hours of sitting in the House of Commons have altered much in the course of centuries. In the seventeenth century a sitting would begin with prayers at 8.30 or 9 in the morning. Difficulties about artificial light discouraged late sittings, and a common form of obstruction was to oppose the order that candles be brought in. In the eighteenth century the adjournment was still nominally till 9 o'clock in the next morning, but business practically began between 3 and 4 in the afternoon. There were late sittings, and it was the rays of the rising sun stealing through the windows of St. Stephen's that once suggested a well-known peroration to the younger Pitt.

After the middle of the nineteenth century the frequency and duration of late sittings told heavily on the health and strength of members, but the burden was mitigated by a new standing order of 1888, the 12 o'clock rule, which terminated ordinary business at midnight. The normal hour for stopping, or, as it is technically called 'interrupting', business was thrown back from 12 to 11 in 1906, so that thereafter it was an 'eleven o'clock' rule that governed the end of the day's sitting. Other changes were made in 1906. The House gave up the dinner interval which, at first informal and short, had been recognized and lengthened by an alteration of the rules in 1902. It also decided to meet at 2.45, instead of at the previous time of 2 p.m., on ordinary sitting days. Towards the end of 1940 the distractions and inconveniences of enemy action, the black-out, and the difficulties of transport caused the hour of meeting to be advanced to 11 a.m., the adjournment being made at 4.30 or, as daylight lengthened, at 5.30 and, later, 6.30 p.m. For reasons of security the dates and hours of sitting were not published. In March 1945 members decided to meet at 2.15 and to adjourn at 9.45 p.m. A year later another half-hour was gained by substituting 2.30 and 10.30 for these times. Some would prefer the House to sit in the morning and leave the evenings free; but this plan would obstruct the use of the morning for making progress with Bills in standing committees. The beginning of Friday sittings at 11 a.m. remains unchanged.

The parliamentary day starts with a dignified little ceremony. The Speaker, preceded by the Serjeant-at-Arms bearing the mace, and followed by his chaplain and his secretary, moves in a stately procession from his quarters in the north of the building to the House for prayers, passing through corridor and lobby. While the Commons temporarily occupy the Lords' chamber, it is a march of some 200 yards. Immediately after prayers the House takes small items of formal business, such as the unopposed stages of Private Bills, motions for unopposed returns, and the presentation of any petitions which members may desire to present orally instead of putting them into an old-fashioned carpet bag at the back of the Speaker's chair. Then follow the asking and answering of questions addressed to ministers, but these must, subject to certain limited exceptions, be finished within the hour, so that the regular business of the day, the public business set down on the notice paper, usually begins shortly before 3.30 and continues until 10.0. After that hour opposed business cannot be taken, unless it belongs to a special 'exempted' class or unless the rule fixing the time for 'interrupting' business has been (as sometimes happens) suspended by order of the House. The category of 'exempted business' includes challenges to 'statutory instruments' when, if the parent Act permits this method of attack, members move a prayer that some Order in Council or other order, rules or regulations made by departments under statutory power may be annulled. At the end of the evening comes another chance for the private member; if he is lucky, he may manage to initiate a short debate on the adjournment. On Fridays the House, having met at 11, and having no question time, does not take opposed business after 4 p.m. or any business after 4.30.

Each House of Parliament has always guarded with great jealousy its own autonomy, its power of regulating its own rights, privileges, and procedure. Hence has grown up the law of parliament of which Sir Edward Coke spoke with so much reverence in the seventeenth century, and which embodies the rights, usages, practice, and regulations of each House. This law consists partly of an unwritten customary law to be gathered from precedents, rulings and decisions, partly of an enacted law to be found in orders of the House. Bentham would have classified it, from another point of view, as a substantive law of rights and privileges, and an adjective law of procedure. The substantive law would include the rules which govern the rights of each House, or of the individual members of each House, in their relations to each other, to the Crown, to the executive and judicial authorities of the country, and to individuals and bodies outside parliament. The privileges which are formally claimed for the House of Commons by its Speaker at the beginning of each parliament bulked large in the seventeenth century controversies between the king and parliament, and were much, and often unreasonably, insisted on by the Commons of the eighteenth century. But in the twentieth century they have retired into the background; questions as to the relations between the two Houses fall under a different category. The cases in which a member of parliament, as such, can now claim any exceptional privilege or immunity, are few and rare. There is naturally a tendency to discourage the assertion of rights which it would be difficult to enforce. 'It has been the practice of the house', once said Mr. Speaker Peel, 'to restrain privilege under great limitations and conditions.'

Into the details of parliamentary procedure this is not the place to enter. There are venerable forms which date from the Plantagenets, such as the mode (already mentioned) of giving the royal assent to Acts, and the Norman-French superscriptions which are placed on Bills when they pass from one house to the other. There are practices which are of great antiquity, but to the origin of which no precise date can be assigned, such as the three readings of Bills. There are rules of etiquette which, from entries in the journals of Sir Symonds d'Ewes, can be traced to the reign of Elizabeth. There are curious survivals which are full of significance to the historical students, such as the formalities observed when leave is given to introduce a Bill into the House of Commons, formalities now occupying a few seconds, but representing, in a compressed and symbolical form, proceedings which, in the seventeenth century may have occupied days or weeks. There is a vast jungle of rulings and precedents in which a veteran member, even a ready and experienced Speaker, may occasionally lose his way. There are a few cases in which, as in the courts of law, mistaken application of precedents seems to have switched procedure from its true course. But the general principles are clear and intelligible enough, and their detailed application is based on the experience of many centuries.

The general principles are such as ought to be observed by all deliberative assemblies. There must be authority to enforce order and decorum, and to prevent waste of time. It is for the convenience of members that they should know what business to expect when they come down to the House, and that they should not be taken by surprise. The unforeseen will often happen in the House of Commons as elsewhere, but there ought to be no unnecessary departure from the programme of the day. Hence the importance of the rules as to notice, rules which often entrap an unwary member, but which were devised and are enforced for the protection of his colleagues. Questions on which the House has to express an opinion must be framed in such a manner as to raise a definite and intelligible issue, and this is the object of the technical rules as to amendments.

The general lines of procedure were fairly settled in the seventeenth century. The tendency of the eighteenth century was to stereotype these rules, and often to encumber them with tedious, intricate, and unnecessary formalities. Rulings and precedents sufficed; Standing Orders, defining and altering practice, were very rare. Of the more than ninety Standing Orders which now regulate the public business of the House of Commons, only three, dealing with finance, date from the eighteenth century, and this is not because the old orders have been repealed but because very few were made. Not until after the Reform Act of 1832 did the need of improving and simplifying the procedure of the House become apparent and urgent. Since that date there have been some twenty committees on the public procedure of the House, besides those devoted to Private Bill procedure; it is on the labours of these committees that the existing Standing Orders of the House are mainly based. It must, however, be repeated that the rules of procedure have never been codified. The Standing Orders do not constitute, and were never intended to constitute, a code. They merely supplement, explain, and alter, in a few particulars, the customary law of the House.

It was the great and rapid growth of parliamentary business, and especially of the business for which the executive government must assume responsibility, that brought the reform of procedure to the forefront after 1832. At a later date the ingenious development of what is known as obstruction made it necessary to confer on the Speaker, the chairman, and the House larger powers of dealing with deliberate efforts to clog the working of the parliamentary machine.

Under the old practice of the House the Speaker and the Chairman of Ways and Means had, and exercised, powers for checking irrelevance, prolixity, repetition, and obstruction, for preventing the abuse of dilatory motions, and for maintaining order and decorum. These are the powers that have now been defined and strengthened by Standing Orders. If a member is guilty of grossly disorderly conduct, the Speaker or the chairman of a committee of the whole House can order him to withdraw from the House. If a member disregards the authority of the chair, or abuses the rules of the House by persistently and wilfully obstructing its business, he can be 'named' for the offence by the Speaker or by the chairman of a committee of the whole House, and the House can, on motion made, make an order suspending him from the service of the House for the rest of the session. Orders of this kind, when made by the House, or by the Speaker or chairman, are enforced, if necessary, by the Serjeant-at-Arms with such assistance as may be required. In the case of grave disorder arising in the House the Speaker may, if he thinks it necessary, adjourn the House without question put, or suspend the sitting.

These, however, are exceptional powers, only exercised in grave and rare emergencies. To facilitate the dispatch of business under normal conditions other Standing Orders have been required and have been made.

It may be stated in general terms that the main problems of parliamentary procedure under existing conditions are two; on the one hand, how to find time within limited parliamentary hours for the growing mass of business which devolves on the Government; and, on the other hand, how to reconcile the legitimate demands of the Government with the legitimate rights of the minority, the dispatch of business with the duties of parliament as a grand inquest of the nation at which all public questions of real importance ought to find opportunity for adequate discussion. These are the problems to the solution of which successive amendments of Standing Orders have been directed.

In the first place, the time appropriated to Government business has been largely increased. Anyone who studies the Standing Orders for the arrangement of public business will find an elaborate scheme prescribed for normal sessions whereunder Wednesdays and Fridays before Easter and certain Fridays after Easter are set aside for the private member 'unless the House otherwise directs'. Unfortunately for the private member, the Government have felt obliged, during a long period of emergency, to persuade the House to direct otherwise. In session after session resolutions have given the Government the whole of his time as well as prohibiting the introduction of any Bills other than Government Bills. By way of compensation he has regularly, since 1943, been allowed half an hour for a debate on the adjournment at the end of the day. This concession soon established itself as a popular means of drawing attention to grievances general or particular. The subject to be discussed is arranged informally in advance and the Ministry concerned has to defend itself. So keenly sought is the chance of initiating these brief debates that the privilege has to be awarded by ballot. If these discussions on the adjournment lead to no decision by the House, they have often elicited some reassuring explanation or sympathetic promise from the Government side. While the private member naturally chafes at the failure to restore to him his former rights of moving motions, it will be remembered that, as explained in a previous chapter, these are not the only, or indeed, the chief opportunities for the exercise of the rights of criticism which belong to private members.

In the next place, it was found necessary to provide machinery for bringing debates to a close by the operation of the closure, a term borrowed from France. Under one of the Standing Orders a member rising in his place may claim to move 'That the question be now put', and, unless it appears to the chair that the motion is an abuse of the rules of the House or an infringement of the rights of the minority, this preliminary question must be put forthwith, and, if it is carried, the original question is put forthwith and decided without amendment or debate. But a motion for the closure cannot be made unless the Speaker or the Chairman or Deputy Chairman of Ways and Means is in the chair, and is not carried unless it appears on a division that not less than 100 members voted in its support. The effect is to leave to the chair much discretion as to the time and circumstances in which closure should, with propriety, be granted.

By subsequent amendments of Standing Orders the machinery of closure was extended to standing committees on Bills. When a Bill is being debated in a committee of the whole House, or at the report stage, the occupant of the chair is now clothed with powers for selecting the particular amendments to be discussed.

In spite of these developments the machinery of the ordinary closure was found inadequate for getting through the most important Government Bills of the session, and, at the instance of, but under protest from, each party in turn, more drastic measures were adopted. They took the form of special orders of the House for the allocation of time on particular Bills, were sometimes described as 'closure by compartments', but have been more popularly known as 'the guillotine'. So much time is allotted for the discussion of a clause or a group of clauses, or a particular stage, of a Bill, and, at the expiration of this time, the necessary question or series of questions is put, all remaining amendments, except Government amendments, being excluded. Attempts are always made so to arrange the time as to afford opportunity for discussing all the more serious issues raised by the Bill, but these attempts are defeated if there is prolongation of debate on minor points. No one defends these orders as satisfactory. Neither party, when in power, has found itself able to do without them. Occasionally, as in the case of the Government of India Bill in 1935, and the Education Bill in 1944, a voluntary time-table has been arranged and successfully operated with general good will.

A considerable amount of time in the House of Commons is occupied by the taking of divisions. The procedure is familiar to those who visit the House. A matter requiring decision is decided by means of a question put from the chair on a motion proposed by a member. When the question arises in the House, or in a committee of the whole House, the Speaker or chairman expresses his opinion as to whether the Ayes or the Noes have it. If his opinion is challenged by dissentient cries, he allows two minutes to elapse, in order to give time for members, who are summoned by the ringing of electric bells, to assemble from other parts of the building, and then puts the question again. If his opinion is again challenged he directs the Ayes to go to the right and the Noes to the left, and appoints two tellers for each. The Ayes and Noes then pass through their respective division lobbies, on each side of the House, their names are taken down by the division clerks, and they are counted by the tellers, who announce the result at the table of the House. With the 'guillotine' at work, the number of possible divisions on a series of questions could be large, and to an outsider the process of tramping through the lobbies in successive divisions, when the result is a foregone conclusion, might seem to be a waste of time. But the experienced member knows better. The intervals allow tempers to cool. Division lists, moreover, are duly chronicled and recorded, and constituents measure the diligence of their member in the performance of his parliamentary duties by the number of divisions in which he takes part. Attendance at an unnecessary division is imputed to him for righteousness, and guillotine nights are useful to him in this way.

The time occupied by a division was somewhat shortened by an improvement of the machinery in 1906, but of course such time-saving arrangements, useful as they are, produce no appreciable effect on the congestion of the business of the House. Some relief has been given by sending Bills 'upstairs' to have their details discussed by what may be called true committees as distinguished from those 'committees of the whole House' which are really the House itself.

During the war of 1939 the Coalition Government confined its law-making to measures necessary for the defeat of the enemy. Its Bills were kept on the floor of the House. Time was also saved by having recourse, as in the war of 1914, to a temporary delegation of wide powers of making emergency regulations by Order in Council and of authorizing departmental orders to be made under those regulations. When victory came, the requirements of a period of reconstruction, not to mention the heavy programme naturally planned by the new Labour administration after its sweeping success at the general election of 1945, stimulated a fresh search for expedients which would speed up the legislative machine. In 1946 the number of Standing Committees upstairs was increased and it was arranged that the Law Officers might attend and assist in all the committee-rooms. The impatient, of course, will still be disappointed. In the case of the class of measures which occupy most time the sending of the Bill upstairs encounters much opposition. The extension of the committee system may impose a heavy strain on members of the House of Commons who are not whole-time politicians. The whips may be conscious that party discipline is less easily maintained in the less spectacular and more co-operative proceedings of a committee-room. It may be harder to preserve a Government majority at the sittings of a committee. A committee of workmanlike size may not be sure of including all the members who wish to contribute to the discussion of a particular Bill; time saved in committee may therefore be lost when the Bill comes back to the House on the report stage. Some reformers advocate a scheme of time limits for speeches; it seems to operate successfully elsewhere. Others believe that preliminary debates on proposals published in a 'white paper' or otherwise will, by elucidating the prospects of support, hasten the passage of the subsequent Bill. Working to a voluntary time-table has produced good results, but fighting on controversial issues is seldom compatible with agreements between the Government and the Opposition. A past generation, having experienced the impact of the Irish party upon the procedure of the House, had great hopes of devolution as the remedy for congestion of business. Here the working of the Northern Ireland government offers material for study. Patriotic Scots and Welshmen demand greater autonomy for their respective countries; it is not clear how far they would surrender the representation of their interests in the Parliament at Westminster. The war-time organization of regional commissioners, planned as a precaution in case communications between London and the provinces should be interrupted, was fortunately not fully tested. Its limited operation, however, disclosed no enthusiasm in the north, south, east, west, or midlands of England for quasi-heptarchical regionalization or for the severance of the accustomed links with the centre.

CHAPTER VII

ORGANIZATION OF THE HOUSE

UNDER THE head of organization two distinct subjects may be legitimately treated. One is the staff of the House, and the constitution of its committees. The other is the arrangements and understandings which regulate the relations of the House to the executive government, and the relations to each other of the political parties and groups represented in the House.

In the earliest days of the House of Commons, when its functions were mainly those of a petitioning body, it needed a spokesman, and some member of the House must have been selected for this purpose. The ordinary list of Speakers begins with Sir Thomas Hungerford, who held the office in the last parliament of Edward III, but there were probably others before him with similar functions. At the beginning of each parliament a member of the House of Commons is elected Speaker of the House; his tenure of office, unless terminated by resignation or death (or, as in Trevor's case in 1695, by expulsion), continues during that parliament. The election is made by the House, subject to the approval of the king, but that approval has never been withheld since Charles II objected to the appointment of Sir Edward Seymour in 1679. In the earlier days of parliament the voice of the king had more influence over the appointment of Speaker; he was regarded as an officer of the king and a link between the king and the House; and in the seventeenth century the conflict between his duties to the king and his duties to the House sometimes placed him in serious difficulties. The emancipation of the Speaker from the control of the king, the severance of his connexion with party during his tenure of office, and the evolution of the non-partisan Speaker, armed with great powers, wielding great authority, and exercising his powers and authority in a judicial and impartial spirit, were admirably described by Edward Porritt in his *Unreformed House of Commons*. The modern Speaker is sometimes elected in the first instance by a party vote, but he is independent of party, his tenure of office is not affected by a change of ministry, and, if he desires to continue his services in a new parliament, the practice (followed in 1945) is to re-elect him, whatever party may be in power. As he stands aside from all political controversy, he is naturally at a great disadvantage in contesting a constituency. There is, however, no definite convention that his return should be unopposed; the elections of 1895, 1935, and 1945 are instances to the contrary.

The Speaker is the representative and spokesman of the House in its collective capacity; he presides at meetings of the House; and he declares and interprets its law. He does not claim power to make or alter that law, merely to be its exponent. But where precedents, rulings, and the orders of the House are insufficient or uncertain guides, he has to consider what course would be most consistent with the usages, traditions, and dignity of the House, and the rights and interests of its members, and on these points his advice is usually followed, and his decisions are very rarely questioned. Much, no doubt, depends on the personal character and qualities of the Speaker, his experience, his readiness, his tact, his knowledge of the ways and habits of members; but for many generations the deference habitually paid to the occupant of the chair has been admired by foreign observers.

The Speaker's symbol of office is the mace. It is carried before him when he formally leaves and enters the House, and remains on the table while he occupies the chair. He has an official residence in the Palace of Westminster, and an official salary which, like the salaries of judges, is not paid out of the votes but is charged on the Consolidated Fund and therefore cannot be questioned when the annual votes are under discussion. When he retires from office he usually receives a pension and a peerage.

Besides the Speaker, two other members of the House of Commons receive salaries as officials of the House. These are the Chairman and the Deputy Chairman of Ways and Means, who ordinarily take the chair at meetings of committees of the whole House, and each of whom can also act as Deputy Speaker during the temporary absence of the Speaker. They are appointed by the House at the beginning of each parliament, for the duration of that parliament. The Chairman of Ways and Means is charged with some important duties in connection with Private Bills. The Deputy Chairman usually presides over committees on unopposed Private Bills.

The House of Commons has its permanent official staff, corresponding to the official staff of the departments of the executive government, the staff which constitutes the permanent civil service of the country. At the head of the staff of clerks is the Clerk of the House, whose office dates from the fourteenth century. He is appointed by the king on the nomination of the Prime Minister. He and the two clerks assistant are the wigged and gowned officials who sit at the table of the House when the Speaker is in the chair, and who are collectively known as the Clerks at the Table. When the Speaker leaves the chair for a sitting of the committee of the whole House, the Clerk of the House has to vacate his seat also, and it is taken by the Chairman of Ways and Means or his deputy. The Serjeant-at-arms, who is also appointed by the king, holds an ancient office in the House and is a picturesque adjunct of its proceedings. But, besides his ceremonial functions, he has responsible duties to perform, and may be treated as representing the executive authority of the House. He sees to the maintenance of order within the precincts of the House, regulates the admission of strangers, and, as housekeeper, looks after its domestic staff and arrangements.

The staff arrangements of the House of Lords are somewhat different. The Lord Chancellor performs the functions assigned in the House of Commons to the Speaker, but (as we shall see presently) has not the same powers for maintaining order and controlling the course of debates. There is a Lord Chairman of Committees, who presides over committees of the whole House, and who exercises considerable control over Private Bill legislation. The Clerk of the Parliaments is the head of the staff of permanent clerks, signifies the assent of the king to legislation, and certifies with his own hand the accuracy of Acts when passed. The Gentleman Usher of the Black Rod, who has a Yeoman Usher to assist him, summons the Commons when their attendance is required in the House of Lords, and performs certain other functions, mostly ceremonial. The Lords, like the Commons, have a Serjeant-at-arms; he carries the mace and attends the Lord Chancellor.

The House of Commons delegates less of its work to committees than legislatures elsewhere, for, as has been previously explained, the so-called 'committees of the whole House' are not committees in the ordinary sense of the term. But much work is done by many genuine committees. These include the standing committees on Public Bills, to which reference has been made in a previous chapter, the select committees on Public Bills or other matters, and the small committees on Private Bills. They also include the sessional committees which the House appoints every session for the transaction of particular branches of its business, such as the Committee of Selection which appoints the members of many committees and makes arrangements for the distribution of their business; the Committee of Public Accounts; the Committee on Publications and Debates Reports; and the Committee on Kitchen and Refreshment Rooms, whose functions require no explanation.

These committees often sit in the mornings during hours when the House is not sitting; attendance at them imposes a severe tax on the time of many members and adds materially to their labours. The work done by them, and especially by their chairmen, is of the highest value, and is appreciated by the House, though it does not come much before the public eye. There is no more useful member of the House than a competent, tactful, and painstaking chairman of committee.

The other aspect of the organization of the House is of greater interest. What is it that makes the House a living organism, instead of a congeries of atoms? What are the forces which discipline its members, and regulate and co-ordinate its daily work? The answers to these questions are to be found in the consideration of the

Cabinet system and the party system, two characteristically English products, which, so far as they exist elsewhere, owe their origin to transplantation from English soil, and which, according to the English view, are inseparable from each other. The stages by which these two systems have grown up in Britain and have developed into their present form, have been described in many admirable treatises, and it is impossible here to do more than glance at some of their leading features.

The great struggle of the seventeenth century between the king and parliament resulted in a compromise, under which executive authority was to remain with the king, but was to be exercised through ministers, having seats in parliament, and depending for their position on the support of the dominant party in the House that provided the supplies without which government could not be carried on. The executive authority, the power of governing the country, was, in fact, put in commission, and it was arranged that the commissioners should be members of the legislative body to whom they are responsible. The process by which this change was carried out has been described as a 'noiseless revolution', and is not to be found embodied in any Acts of Parliament. It may be said to have begun under William III between 1693 and 1696, but it extended over a long period of time. In its early stages (as has already been explained in our chapter on the constitution of the House) experiments were made, such as the exclusion of office-holders from parliament, experiments which, if they had succeeded, would have resulted in the establishment of an entirely different system, more resembling that set up afterwards in the United States.

The process was expedited by the fact that during

nearly half a century the throne was occupied by kings who were foreigners in their origin, in their habits, in their modes of thought, in their interests, and in their language, and who were therefore compelled to rely on, and to act through, ministers drawn from and representing the views of the great English families who had been mainly instrumental in bringing them over. George III, who was born and bred in England, and trained by a Scot, did not labour under similar disadvantages, and succeeded for some years in re-establishing, by indirect means, a system of personal government by the king. But the reins dropped from his hands long before the end of his life, and have not been taken back by his successors. The king, as an individual, has, in the region of executive government, receded into the background. His office remains as a potent symbol of dignity, authority, and continuity, and as a link between the various parts of the British Commonwealth and Empire. In his individual capacity he can exercise enormous influence by wise and timely counsel. But he is not responsible for the acts or defaults of his ministers. If he should thrust his personal authority into the foreground he would throw the machine out of gear.

What is now called the Cabinet system of government was first described, accurately and graphically, by Walter Bagehot in Lord Palmerston's time, and the main lines of his description still hold good. The system thus described was built up, not by legislation, but by understandings and conventions, is always liable to modification, and assumes different aspects from different points of view. Queen Victoria was an admirable constitutional sovereign, but it is very doubtful whether she would ever have accepted Bagehot's theory of the constitution.

The essential features of the Cabinet system of government, those which distinguish it from the presidential system of the United States, are that the king's principal ministers, the men who are responsible for the government of the country, must be members of parliament, and must resign office if they are unable to command the confidence of the dominant party in the House of Commons. They are the link between the executive authority and the legislative authority. On the one hand they are the king's ministers, exercising their powers in the king's name, and it is by them, and not by either House of Parliament, or by any committee of either House, that the government of the country is carried on. On the other hand, they are members of the legislature, liable at any moment, so long as parliament is sitting, to be called to account for their actions by the House to which they belong, and dependent for their tenure of office, technically on the king's pleasure, but practically on the good will of the House of Commons. The most important of these ministers constitute the Cabinet, a body of perhaps twenty persons, having the Prime Minister as their chief. The Cabinet has been described as a committee, but, if this description is to be accepted, it is a very informal and anomalous committee. It is not a committee of either House of Parliament, or a joint committee of the two Houses, for it is not appointed by and does not report its proceedings to either House. The members of the Cabinet must be members of the Privy Council, and thus the Cabinet may be treated as a committee of Privy Councillors. But it is not a committee of the Privy Council, for it is not appointed by and does not report its proceedings to that body. In fact the Cabinet does not report its proceedings at all. Its meetings are private, and are held usually in Downing Street, but often at other places, such as the Prime Minister's room in the House of Commons. It has a secretary (appointed for the first time in 1919) and keeps records of its proceedings, but treats them as matters of secrecy which it is a breach of confidence for any member of its body to divulge except by permission of its chief. The Prime Minister, who is the chief of the Cabinet, is appointed by the king, but the king's selection is practically limited to some one of a very small number of persons. The person selected must be capable of leading the political party to which he belongs, and the selection is often indicated by the public opinion of the country. The other members of the Cabinet, being the king's ministers, are also appointed by him, and, technically, may be dismissed by him. But they are practically selected by the Prime Minister, who takes care to choose persons who are likely to command the confidence of his party and to conduct the business of the Government efficiently in parliament. If a member of the Cabinet, or a minister who is not in the Cabinet, finds himself unable to reconcile his political opinions on some vital point with those of his chief, he resigns his office; a minister whose conduct or action has incurred the disapproval of parliament has sometimes been compelled to resign. The Melbourne papers have made it clear that the retirement of the Melbourne ministry in 1834 was not a case of dismissal by the exercise of the king's personal will.

What is called the solidarity of the Cabinet, by which is meant their collective responsibility for the acts and defaults of individual members of their body, and the special responsibility of the Prime Minister, as their chief, for their acts, and even for their words, is a principle which has been developed by a process of slow growth, and the application of which is still liable to be a matter of controversy and doubt. Much depends on personal character, time, and circumstances. There have been times when a powerful personality, like that of Peel, has dominated and controlled the administration in all its branches. At other times the Prime Minister's reins have been held more loosely, and the work of government has tended to fall into separate, almost watertight, compartments. There have been grave questions which have been treated as open because the members of the Cabinet could not come to an agreement about them. On other questions, the extent to which a member of the Cabinet should, in the public interest, subordinate his convictions to those of his chief or his colleagues is a matter for the individual conscience. If the strain is too severe, the Cabinet may shed some of its members, as in 1867 and again in 1903. But, speaking generally, it is considered to be the duty of members of the Cabinet, and of members of the Government who are outside the Cabinet, to present a united front in dealing with all the more important questions that come before parliament.

The ministry, the Cabinet, must govern. But how can they control the body on whose favour their existence depends? How can they prevent the House of Commons from being an unorganized, uncontrollable, irresponsible mob? The English answer is, by party machinery. It is this machinery that secures the necessary discipline. The Cabinet system presupposes a party system, and, more than that, a two-party system. This does not mean that there may not be individual members of the legislature independent of party, or that there may not be more than two parties in each House. But it does mean that there must be two main parties, one represented by the Treasury Bench, the bench on which the ministers sit, and the other by the front opposition bench, and that the party represented by the Treasury bench must be able, with or without its allies, to control the majority of the House of Commons. Without party, said Disraeli, parliamentary government is impossible. The system also implies, for its efficient working, an experienced and responsible opposition, a body of men whose leaders have held office in the past and may look forward to holding office in the future. The phrase 'His Majesty's Opposition', which was invented by John Cam Hobhouse (Lord Broughton) in the early part of the last century, means a body of men who may, if the balance of party power shifts, become, or be willing to succeed, His Majesty's ministers. As already mentioned, the Ministers of the Crown Act 1937 went so far as to provide a statutory salary for the Leader of the Opposition.

In the eighteenth century and later, the 'influence' which held the dominant party together and secured their votes, took the gross and material form of places and bribes. The methods have been changed, but traces of them still remain. It is said that an intelligent foreigner, anxious to obtain information about the working of our parliamentary system, recently asked a minister what was the official title of the person described to him as the chief Government whip. 'The patronage secretary of the Treasury' was the reply. 'Ah,' he said, with a sagacious smile, 'now I understand, you need not tell me any more.' Of course he was under a misapprehension, but intelligent foreigners are full of half-knowledge.

What does the expression 'whip' mean in parliamentary language, and what is its origin? The metaphor is borrowed from the hunting-field, and its parliamentary application can be traced to Burke. In May 1769 there was a great debate in the House of Commons on the petition against the return of Colonel Luttrell for Westminster in the place of Alderman Wilkes, who had been expelled from the House by its order. The king's ministers made great efforts to bring their followers together from all quarters for this debate. Burke, who took part in the debate, referred to these efforts, and described how ministers had sent for their friends to the north and to Paris, whipping them in, than which, he said, there could not be a better phrase. The phrase thus adopted and commended by Burke caught the public fancy and soon became popular. In the Annual Register of 1772 we find a sketch of an imaginary politician of whom it is said that 'he was first a whipper-in to the Premier, and then became Premier himself'. Whipper-in was ultimately abbreviated into whip.

The whips are the agents through whom party machinery is used for the conduct of the business of the House. They are the eyes and ears of their party chief. It is their business to try and discern the direction in which sections of opinion are moving, to hear any mutterings of discontent, and to suggest methods for mitigating or removing it.

The Government whips are paid officials, with official titles which do not indicate their real work. The chief of them is a Secretary of the Treasury, others are junior lords of the Treasury, and one of them often holds a post in the King's Household. They have an office in Downing Street besides their official rooms at the House of Commons. They perform important duties in connexion with the arrangement of the business of the House. They sketch out a forecast of the probable work of the session, or of a part of the session, estimating the time which each item of work will occupy and how much time can be spared for it. The chief whip settles, under instructions from the Prime Minister, the programme of Government business for each sitting of the House of Commons, and sees that the necessary notices are handed in at the table of the House. He ascertains, by communication with the whips of the other parties, what kind of opposition the items on the programme are likely to encounter, and how many and which of them have a reasonable chance of being reached and disposed of before the end of the sitting. He also arranges in the same way the days on which it would be most convenient to take particular votes of supply, and how committees appointed by the House through the Committee of Selection will best represent various sections and interests. These are the arrangements which are referred to when members of either of the two front benches talk of communications passing through the usual channels. It is by means of arrangements and understandings of this kind, carried on through the agency of the Government whips, that a great part of the business of the House is conducted; it could not be got through in any other manner.

The regular opposition, whose leaders are on the front opposition bench, and any other parties outside the ranks of the Government's supporters, have whips of their own, but without the advantage of official posts or official salaries.

During the session the whips of the several parties

send round weekly notices, also sometimes called 'whips', warning the members of their party when important divisions are expected, telling them at what hour the division will probably take place, and expressing a hope that they will be in attendance at that time. The relative gravity of the prospective occasion is marked by the number of lines—one, two, or three—with which the message is underscored. If a member wishes to withdraw from his party, he signifies his desire not to receive these notices from its whip. He may, of course, if he pleases, declare his independence of party by declining to receive any party whip. By so doing he sometimes increases his chance of a hearing in the House, but usually endangers his seat.

These party arrangements make it easier for a member to perform his parliamentary duties. He cannot be expected to be always in the House itself; he has quite enough to occupy him in the committee room, in the library, in the smoking-room or elsewhere. But when the division bell rings he hurries into the House, and is told by his whip whether he is an 'Aye' or a 'No'. When a division takes place on party lines, the party whips act as tellers. When they do not, members understand and, if necessary, are told by their whips that they can vote as they please, without regard to party obligations. Requests that members may be thus freed from party obligations are not infrequently made. There are occasions when they can be properly and usefully granted. But it may be doubted whether open questions are really popular. A House is never more interesting than when members are left free to vote according to their individual consciences and convictions, and never more puzzled. Each member has to think and decide for himself, which is always troublesome. Not that a member is a mere pawn in the game; far from it, but the number of questions which even a member of parliament has leisure and capacity to think out for himself is necessarily limited. And it is only through machinery of the kind described that a member of parliament can reconcile his independence as a rational being with the efficiency of a disciplined and organized body.

It is not merely, and indeed not mainly, through the action of the whips that party discipline is maintained. The pressure of public opinion, and of the opinion of constituents in particular, makes itself felt in many ways, and is, as a rule, adverse to those who wobble and to those who are slack. When in 1836 the division lists were first regularly published, their publication elicited a protest from some old-fashioned members against what they regarded as the imposition of shackles on their independence. In the present day the division lists are jealously scrutinized and carefully analysed, and the member who is slack in attendance or uncertain in his allegiance is apt to be called to account by his constituents.

CHAPTER VIII

THE MEMBER AND HIS CONSTITUENTS

WHAT ARE the duties of a member of the House of Commons? By what obligations is he bound to the constituency by which he is returned and to the political party to which he is attached? What kind of work is he expected to do, and what kind of life has he to lead? We may try to answer these questions, first by referring to some general principles, and then by giving a concrete illustration.

In November 1774 Edmund Burke was invited at short notice to stand for one of the two vacant seats at Bristol. He was a stranger to the place, but his colleague was a local gentleman of accommodating nature, who expressed his willingness to carry out any instructions which he might receive from his constituents. Burke was duly elected, and in his subsequent address to the electors he touched on the topic of instructions to members. This is what he said—

'Certainly, gentlemen, it ought to be the happiness and glory of a representative to live in the strictest union, the closest correspondence, and the most unreserved communication with his constituents. Their wishes ought to have great weight with him; their opinion high respect; their business unremitted attention. It is his duty to sacrifice his repose, his pleasures, his satisfactions, to theirs; and above all, ever, and in all cases, to prefer their interest to his own. But, his unbiased opinion, his mature judgment, his enlightened conscience, he ought not to sacrifice to you, to any man, or to any set of men living. These he does not derive from your pleasure; no, nor from the law and the constitution. They are a trust from Providence, for the abuse of which he is deeply answerable. Your representative owes you, not his industry only, but his judgment; and he betrays, instead of serving you, if he sacrifices it to your opinion.

'My worthy colleague says his will ought to be subservient to yours. If that be all, the thing is innocent: if government were a matter of will upon my side, yours, without question, ought to be superior. But government and legislation are matters of reason and judgment, and not of inclination; and what sort of reason is that, in which the determination precedes the discussion; in which one set of men deliberate, and another decide; and where those who form the conclusion are perhaps three hundred miles distant from those who hear the arguments?

'To deliver an opinion, is the right of all men; that of constituents is a weighty and respectable opinion, which a representative ought always to rejoice to hear, and which he ought always most seriously to consider. But authoritative instructions, mandates issued, which the member is bound blindly and implicitly to obey, to vote and to argue for, though contrary to the clearest conviction of his judgment and conscience—these are things utterly unknown to the laws of the land, and which arise from a fundamental mistake of the whole order and tenor of our constitution.

'Parliament is not a congress of ambassadors from different and hostile interests; which interests each must maintain, as an agent, and advocate, against other agents and advocates; but parliament is a deliberative assembly of one nation, with one interest, that of the whole; where, not local purposes, not local prejudices, ought to guide, but the general good, resulting from the general reason of the whole. You choose a member indeed: but when you have chosen him, he is not a member of Bristol, but he is a member of parliament.'

This passage has become classical. The principles laid down by Burke were not novel, for they had been previously enunciated by Blackstone and others, but they had never been so eloquently or forcibly expressed. Despite the differences between the eighteenth century and the twentieth century, differences enormous both in the character of the constituencies and in the position of the members returned, these principles would probably be accepted by most members of parliament as sound at the present day. A member of parliament is elected by a local constituency, he has special duties towards it; but he is not a mere delegate or mouthpiece; he is a member of a body which is responsible for the interests of the country at large, and, though he is influenced by the wishes and views of his constituents and by the action of his party, he does not surrender his right of independent judgement.

In the earliest days of parliamentary history the ties which bound a member to his constituents were much closer than they are at present. There were several reasons for this. The work of the House of Commons was less important; the functions of the Commons were mainly to present petitions for the redress of grievances and to grant taxes; they had not yet become responsible for the administration of the country. Parliaments were short. Members were required to be resident in their constituencies. They received wages from their constituents. Thus they were much in the position of paid agents of, or delegates from, particular bodies or communities, and it is not surprising that in 1339, when the Commons were asked to grant an aid asked for by the king, they replied that they could not do so without consulting the commons of the country, and for this purpose, desired that another parliament be summoned. In the fifteenth century it seems to have been the practice for borough members to address their electors and give an account of their proceedings when presenting their bills for wages and travelling expenses, so that there are ancient precedents for the addresses which twentieth-century members are expected to deliver periodically to their constituents.

Prynne, writing at a time when the receipt of wages by members had not yet become quite obsolete, says that

'wages begot a greater confidence, correspondence and dependence between knights, citizens and burgesses, and those who elected and defrayed their expenses, than when or where no wages or expenses were demanded and received as due by law, and gave the electors who paid just occasion to check them or detain their wages in case of abuse, neglect, or unnecessary protraction of their sessions.'

The last person known to have received wages regularly as a member was Andrew Marvell, the poet. He was member for Hull during the first eighteen years of Charles II's reign, having been returned, not by the people of Hull, but by the mayor and aldermen; and he richly earned his wages by sending regularly, almost to the day of his death, letters to his good friend the mayor, conveying information about proceedings in parliament, and about London affairs generally. In fact he did for them the kind of work now done by the London correspondent of a local newspaper. We find him asking for instructions as to how he should act.

'I desire that you will, now being the time, consider whether there be anything that particularly relates to the state of your town, or of your neighbouring country, or of yet more public concernment, whereof you may think fit to advertise me, and therein to give me any your instructions, to which I shall carefully conform.'

Instructions of this kind were common in the eighteenth century. Most of the English boroughs sent instructions to their members to oppose Walpole's unpopular Excise Bill of 1733. When such instructions enjoined a policy distasteful to the Crown, they were often countered by 'loyal addresses', the cost of obtaining which was sometimes paid by the king or his ministers. Burke's speech of 1774 seems to have sent 'instructions' out of fashion. Other modes of influencing parliamentary action remained or grew up, but this particular mode disappeared.

After the great change effected by the Reform Act of 1832, precise instructions, such as Marvell asked for and received, were no longer practicable. After that time members ceased to be nominees of individual patrons, or of a little knot of men, such as a mayor and a dozen aldermen; they became representatives of larger and more popular constituencies, whose views and wishes had to be ascertained and formulated in a different manner.

The Redistribution Act of 1885, which was based on the principle of splitting up the country into approximately equal electoral districts, weakened, if it did not destroy, the old corporate character of constituencies, and strengthened the view that a member represents the country as a whole, and that it is merely for the convenience of election that the country is divided into electoral districts.

The modern tendency is to make an election turn, not on local questions or local interests, but on general questions which agitate the country at large. The voters may in effect be expressing their opinions for or against a particular leader. A candidate usually comes forward either as the supporter or as the opponent of the Government of the day, and is expected to give a general pledge that he will act as a member of, and in accordance with the general policy of, some one of the great political parties in parliament. He may be harassed by demands for pledges on particular questions, such as temperance or the position of trades unions, and hampered by such pledges as he gives in response to these demands. He is expected to shape his course in parliament in conformity, or at all events consistently, with the pledges thus given, and sits, less as the representative of a particular locality, than as a member of the political party which has obtained a majority of votes in that locality. He owes allegiance to his party, and to the leaders of that party. He is in no sense a mere delegate or agent, whose powers are limited and whose authority can be withdrawn. If, after his election, he should change his party, he could not be required to resign his seat. Political parties in this country are not divided from each other by any unbridgeable gulf; they shade into each other, and it is often on a balance of competing and conflicting considerations that a man makes up his mind to attach himself to one party rather than to another. Change of circumstances or change of opinion may alter that balance, and compel him to reconsider his position. If on such reconsideration he come to the conclusion that he can no longer properly act with the political party in which he is enrolled, he does not necessarily incur blame; he may even be entitled to praise, for it is not without a severe wrench that a public man severs his political ties. What a member of parliament has to consider in such a case is, how far his future course of action will be consistent with the promises which he has made to his constituents and with the expectations on the faith of which he was elected. When a member has made up his mind to cross the floor of the House and join another set of political allies, he sometimes offers to resign his seat and submit himself for re-election, in order to ascertain whether his action meets with the approval of the majority of his constituents. But he is not bound to do this, it is merely a question of conduct, of propriety, which he must settle for himself.

Though efforts are made to reduce the expense of contesting a constituency, few sitting members welcome a general election. Their leaders therefore can insist on support as a token of the confidence which maintains the party in power. It has been said that party organization in parliament has become stricter in recent years. But in the common talk about party tyranny, and about the despotism exercised by Cabinets or whips, there is, to speak plainly, much nonsense and much cant. A member of parliament is not a puppet, but a human being, very human, influenced by the same kind of considerations and actuated by the same kind of motives as his fellow mortals outside the walls of the House. He recognizes the importance of combination and organization in politics, as in the other affairs of life; he is willing to subordinate, on many points, his individual preferences and opinions to those of his leaders; he knows that debate is team-work and that he must submit to discipline if he is to be an effective member of an organized body. But no one knows better than a political leader what arts of persuasion, what tactics of conciliation and compromise, are required to keep a party together. He knows that too severe a strain must not be put on party allegiance, that diversity of opinions within the party ranks must be recognized, and that on many points the lines of division between different opinions by no means coincide with the lines of division between different political parties. And leaders and followers alike are aware that they cannot afford to disregard public opinion outside parliament, that they must watch its variations and fluctuations, and guide their actions accordingly. Indeed, the chief risk is that they should be too sensitive to currents and gusts of so-called public opinion, as indicated in the fallacious weather chart of the press.

Despotic or arbitrary rule, and rigidity of discipline, are quite incompatible with the position of a member of parliament. He has to act under a variety of influences and motives, often pulling in different directions. In the lobbies and in the smoking-room he is brought into constant and friendly contact and intercourse not only with his political friends but with his political opponents, and has opportunities for ascertaining their views, and also for influencing their opinions and actions. He may be, from the whips' point of view, a troublesome member and uncomfortably independent, apt to bolt, always to be watched, and often to be soothed. Or he may be a 'safe' member, one who can be counted on to vote straight, who is not often heard in debate, but who has acquired a reputation for sound judgement, and whose warnings and advice always command respect. But, in any case, he is a member of a body receptive of and responsible to many diverse and quickly changing influences from within and from without, and incapable of being drilled into mechanical action.

During the session the immediate relations of a member are mainly with his colleagues in the House. But he is not only a member of parliament, he is also a member for a particular constituency, and his relations to his constituents, whether they have voted for him at the poll or not, are constant and close, and require unremitting attention both in and out of session and both at Westminster and elsewhere. He may be a local magnate, a man of high social position in the country, a member of a family whose name and influence have for generations been weighty in the neighbourhood. He may be a great employer of local labour. He may have made himself well and favourably known by successful administration of local affairs. He may have acquired the confidence of working men as the secretary or guiding spirit of an important union or industrial organization. He may be a stranger, who owes his seat to his own ability or reputation, or to the efforts, oratorical or other, of his friends. He may have 'nursed' the constituency for months or years, and devoted much time, labour, and money to this purpose. He may be a speaker whose voice and personality have been projected into the homes of the people by the British Broadcasting Corporation, so that he seems to need no further introduction. But, whatever he is, he will find, when he enters the House, that his duties to his constituents are absorbing and exhausting. Mere correspondence will impose a severe tax on his time. The days when Andrew Marvell could discharge his obligations by writing a weekly letter to his 'worthy friends', the mayor and aldermen of Hull, are long past. Modern constituencies are great multitudes, who use their pens freely, and expect replies. The modern member may receive as many as two hundred letters a week; many of them may involve him in a reference to the appropriate department. Indeed a single letter may cause him a protracted correspondence which will not always end in a message of gratitude. The topics will vary from political issues to personal troubles over demobilization, re-employment, pensions, housing, and even matrimonial difficulties. The State gives neither free postage (save in addressing a Government department) nor secretarial help. He has to spend his mornings in dictating letters, and his afternoons and evenings in writing them in the library and lobbies of the House of Commons. He is expected to ask questions in the House about matters of local interest, and to communicate by post the ministerial reply, with such comments as occur to him. Under Queen Elizabeth the House of Commons required members to give special attention to what would now be called Local Bills affecting the constituency The House was 'not to go to the question of any such Bill, if it concerned a town or shire, unless the knights of such shire or shires, or the burgesses of such town or towns, be then present'. The modern rule works in the opposite direction, for the existing Standing Orders require a member of a committee on an opposed Private Bill to sign a declaration, not only that he has no personal interest, but that his constituents have no local interest, in the Bill. The reason is that these committees act judicially, and that their members must, like judges, be above suspicion of interest or bias. Nevertheless, if a Private Bill comes up for discussion on general principles in the House, a member is permitted, and is often expected, to explain how its passing or rejection would affect the interests or welfare of the constituency which he represents, and to argue for or against it accordingly. And, if the Bill be not Private but Public, proposing a change in the general law, each member is bound to consider how the proposals will affect the constituents, or any important section of the constituents, for whose welfare he is specially responsible, and to pay close attention to any representations made to him on the subject. These representations will be made to him, not merely by correspondence, but by means of deputations and personal conferences, and, although a private member is not so much beset by deputations as a minister, yet he may have, in the course of the session, to receive many deputations and take part in many conferences on his own account, and to convey, through deputations or personal interviews, the wishes and opinions of his constituents to the ministers who are responsible for the government and legislation of the country. Nor will his duties to his constituency be exhausted by attention to their legislative and administrative requirements. He has to be courteous and obliging to individual constituents, and to their wives and children. He may be beset with applications for admission to the galleries, especially on days when an exciting or important debate is expected. He may be seen conducting friends of either sex, with whom his relations are political rather than social, through the corridors of the House, or (if such amenities be possible) entertaining them on the Terrace, or personally conducting a numerous and happy band of schoolboys or schoolgirls.

Such are the duties of a member to his constituents whilst he is at Westminster. But his duties elsewhere, whether during a week-end or during such other intervals as he may snatch from the performance of his strictly parliamentary work, or during the longer recesses, will be numerous and various. He will have to give periodical addresses to his constituents, reviewing the proceedings in parliament, and justifying his own share in them. There will be meetings, social, charitable, and political, which he will have to attend, and at many of which he will have to take the chair. There will be lectures on improving or popular subjects to deliver. There may not be so many bazaars to open or garden parties to attend as in the Victorian age. Writing of those times in retrospect in his volumes on *The Public Life*, J. A. Spender remarked that later generations could never quite realize the awe which surrounded the old politics, the respect with which the member was received when he visited his constituents, his affable condescension, the air of mystery with which he spoke of his parliamentary duties, his admired incompetence in public speaking, his long words and rotund phrases and the deep pauses while he consulted his notes. Those were the days when an assiduous candidate could hope to become personally known to a large part of his constituents. If this intimate association is now scarcely possible, the local member is still in request for many purposes and occasions. His life is one of strenuous and multifarious activity. He often complains of the way in which his time is wasted at the House of Commons. There are tedious hours during which he is waiting for a threatened division, while bores are making dull speeches, or time is being frittered away over petty details. There are anxious hours, when he is sitting in an expectant attitude on the edge of a bench in the House, with a bundle of notes on his lap, waiting to catch the Speaker's eye, and to deliver a speech the points of which are being anticipated from other lips, and which may never be delivered at all. But there are times of interest and excitement, when history is being made, and when he feels that he is an active participant in its making. Members who are in the House often doubt whether a career which for many seems to mean wasted energies, fruitless endeavours, and baffled hopes is worth the sacrifice involved; but members who have left the House usually look wistfully back.

Sir George Trevelyan, in his *Life of Macaulay*, has depicted the less attractive side of parliamentary life as it presented itself in 1853:

> 'The tedious and exhausting routine of a political existence; waiting whole evenings for the vote, and then walking half a mile at a foot's pace round and round the crowded lobbies; dining amidst clamour and confusion, with a division of twenty minutes long between two of the mouthfuls; trudging home at three in the morning through the slush of a February thaw; and sitting behind ministers in the centre of a closely packed bench during the hottest weeks of a London summer.'

Much the same picture could be presented forty years later by Sir Richard Temple's *Life in Parliament*, the story of six years of industrious membership during which the author took part in 2,072 out of 2,118 possible divisions. But we are considering the members in their relation to their constituents rather than in relation to their surroundings in the House. Of the modern aspects it may suffice to say that the broadening of the franchise and of the public interest in parliament has given constituencies a greater zest for studying the speeches and the activities of their member and has incited them to make more use of him, even though, when they read their newspapers, the item of parliamentary news may be the last to attract their eye. The popular press indeed may offer them only a partial and scanty account of what goes on in the Palace of Westminster. Up to 1890 or thereabouts, wrote J. A. Spender, the newspapers lay under the old tradition. They spoke with awe of parliament and recorded its proceedings in whole pages of solid type. The press followed the politicians from the House to the platform with the same respectful tender of its services and the same voluminous reporting. But by the nineties the time had come when a new type of newspaper proprietor emerged and asked whether this stuff was read, whether it was 'copy', whether any human being who was not a professional politician could honestly say that he liked it or wanted it or did anything with it except turn from it with a sigh to the report of a murder or a fire. 'Parliament, unless it provided a "scene", was reduced to half a column of small type, and the claims of the great, wise and eminent to occupy space urgently required for crime and football was openly derided.' From that twilight of publicity the House of Commons has been rescued by the summaries and commentaries broadcast by wireless transmission to every home. Stimulated by the energetic efforts of the Hansard Society, the sales of the reports of parliamentary debates are expanding; to those who have the leisure and the patience to read them in full, they offer the only impartial account of the manner in which members represent and serve their constituents.

CHAPTER IX

RECORDS, THE PRESS, AND THE PUBLIC

THE HOUSE OF COMMONS possesses no early records of historical value except the old manuscript Journals of the House. Three of these volumes, that with the page of protestation torn out by James I in 1621, that with the unfinished entry as to the attempted arrest of the five members in 1642, and that with the erased entry as to the dispersion of the Long Parliament by Cromwell in 1650, are on show in the Members' Library. The other manuscript volumes are now in the Public Record Office. Such original documents as early writs of summons, parliament and statute rolls, and old Bills and Acts, are mostly to be found either in the Record Office, or in the Victoria Tower, which adjoins the House of Lords. They relate, not only to the House of Lords, but to parliament as a whole.

The chief official records of the proceedings of parliament are, for the period down to the end of Henry VII's reign, the rolls of parliament, and, for the later period, the Journals of the two Houses.

The contents of the rolls of parliament are to be found in six folio volumes which were printed in pursuance of orders given by the House of Lords in 1767; an index volume was added in 1832. The earliest entries in these volumes relate to the parliament of 1278, the latest to the parliament of 1503; but at the beginning of the first volume there are some supplemental entries, relating to the period from 1513 to 1553, and intended to supply deficiencies in the Lords Journals for that period.

The nature of the proceedings in the earliest parliaments has been described in our first chapter, and it will have been seen that the business related mainly to petitions for the redress of grievances, by legislation or otherwise. The bulk of the entries in the rolls of parliament consists of these petitions, with short notes of the replies. There are also a few records of the pleas held in the High Court of Parliament, acting in its judicial capacity. And there are descriptions of the formal proceedings at the opening of parliament. During the earlier period some of the more important of the parliamentary enactments were occasionally entered on the rolls, but it was not until the reign of Richard III that Acts of Parliament were regularly so enrolled. At a later date the petitions gradually dropped out, and only Acts were entered.

The Journals of the House of Lords begin in 1509, but are not complete for the whole of Henry VIII's reign. At that time the House of Commons had no fixed habitation, but found precarious lodging in the Chapter House at Westminster or elsewhere. It was not until 1547 that they obtained permanent quarters in St. Stephen's Chapel, and that is the date at which the extant Journals of the House of Commons begin. We happen to know that at an earlier date their clerk recorded entries in a book, but all such records are lost. The Commons Journals for the years from 1581 to 1603 have also been lost. The series of manuscripts on which the printed edition is based was made up towards the end of the seventeenth century, and there is reason to believe that the original manuscripts were dispersed or destroyed during the Great Rebellion.

The earlier Journals of each House are of an experimental character, and are enlivened by a personal note which vanished when the forms of entry became stereotyped. John Taylor, who kept the first Journals of the House of Lords in Henry VIII's reign, incidentally tells us various things about himself and his opinions. He was not only Clerk of Parliaments but also Prolocutor of Convocation. He enters the fact that the Earl of Wiltshire had freely and without solicitation, and in the presence of four witnesses, granted to him the presentation to the next vacancy in the living of Skyrby, in Lincolnshire. He describes in terms of exuberant eloquence how Mr. Thomas Neville acquitted himself so well on presenting himself as Speaker that the king knighted him then and there. His entries are mainly in Latin, but he occasionally breaks into the vernacular, as where he makes a memorandum that 'It is agreed by the Lords that stockfishmongers and fishmongers be warned to be here on Thursday next by 9 of the clock.'

The earliest entries in the Commons Journals are short and barren, and contain little more than the successive stages of different Bills. Then come narratives, brief at first, but gradually expanding, of the formalities at the opening and the close of a session. The Journal of 1562 gives as a reason for putting off the ceremony at the opening of Queen Elizabeth's second parliament that 'the Queen's Majesty was somewhat sick of a styche'. The record of proceedings in the course of a session also expands into something more than mere entries of Bills. When the Commons were exhorting Queen Elizabeth to marry, we are told how she sent them a peremptory command not to proceed further in the matter, and how Mr. Speaker recited a commandment from the Queen's Majesty to spend little time in motions and to avoid long speeches. Orders as to procedure are noted from time to time. Questions of privilege crop up, and much space is devoted to Mr. Arthur Hall and his 'lewd speeches'. He seems to have 'charged this House with drunkenness, as accompanied in their counsels by Bacchus' and he had to expiate his offences by fine and imprisonment. In the reign of James I the entries in the Commons Journals become more copious, and the personal note of the journalist is more prominent. The clerk makes an entry that on one occasion during the argument on a Bill, a young jackdaw flew into the house, and called 'malum omen'. He tells us a good deal about a solemn feast which he attended at Merchant Taylors' Hall with the Speaker, and how he presented the feast with a 'marchpane' (a kind of cake), representing the House of Commons sitting. He does his best to take rough notes of speeches made in the House, but often does not succeed in getting down much more than the Latin and biblical catchwords and quotations with which the speeches of that time were plentifully interlarded. But this practice of taking at the table notes of debate, however useful it might be to the future historian, was destined soon to be checked and stopped. James I had an inconvenient habit of sending for the Commons Journals and perusing their contents, and we know how on one occasion he tore out an offending page with his own hand. Strong protests were made against disclosure of the proceedings of the House, and eventually, but not until the following reign, the question was settled by a resolution of the House in 1628 that the entry by the clerk of particular men's speeches was without warrant. In 1640 the 'Short Parliament' emphasized this resolution by another, directing that Mr. Rushworth, who had then been appointed clerk assistant, 'shall not take any notes here without the precedent direction and commands of this House, but only of the orders and reports of this House'. Since then the record kept by the clerks at the table of the House of Commons, and entered in the Journals, has, with a few formal exceptions, been confined to things done, as distinguished from things said, and the report of parliamentary debates has to be sought elsewhere.

Whilst the scope of the Journal was limited by the suppression of notes of speeches, it tended to expand in other directions with the growing business of the House, and had to be supplemented, before long, by other official records.

In 1680 the House of Commons, by resolution, authorized the printing and distribution to members of minutes of the daily Votes and Proceedings, and this practice has continued ever since, under an order of the House which is made, as a matter of course, at the beginning of each session.

The bulk and variety of the papers circulated with the 'Votes and Proceedings', and the mass of papers thus supplied to each member of the House of Commons daily during the session, has now become formidable. They include the agenda for the day, and also Bills, notices of amendments, notices of questions, division lists, and many other matters.

The short notes of proceedings taken by the clerks of each House, while sitting at the table, and circulated next morning in a printed form, are subsequently elaborated into the official Journals of the House. Reports made to either House and papers presented to it were occasionally inserted in the Journals from a very early date, and in the course of the seventeenth century papers of this kind were from time to time printed and published by order of the House. The number of these papers grew in the eighteenth century, and in the year 1773 a selection was made of valuable reports of committees not printed in the Journals. The four volumes thus formed were supplemented in 1803 by eleven additional volumes, making fifteen in all, with an index. This became the nucleus of the vast collection of parliamentary papers, popularly called 'blue books', which has been continued to the present day, and which lines so many shelves in the libraries and galleries of the two Houses of Parliament. It comprises more than 7,000 folio volumes; the series for 1908 alone consists of 126 volumes and covers twenty-five feet of shelf-space. These volumes, nowadays in octavo form and less numerous because many documents formerly published as parliamentary papers now appear as Stationery Office publications, are arranged at the end of each session under four general heads: 1. Public Bills; 2. Reports from Committees; 3. Reports from Commissions; 4. Accounts and Papers. The last of these heads includes the numerous returns which are presented to parliament either in pursuance of special orders of the House of Commons or of standing directions in Acts of Parliament. There are general indexes to these parliamentary papers for the two periods 1801–52 and 1852–99, and these are supplemented by annual and decennial indexes. The documents included in this collection are, it need hardly be said, indispensable, not only to historical students, but to the executive departments of the Government, and to those who are actively concerned in legislation and administration throughout the British Commonwealth and Empire.

The orders passed by the House of Commons in 1628 and 1640, forbidding their clerks to take notes of speeches, effected a complete divorce between the official records of parliamentary proceedings and the records of parliamentary debates.

From 1628, when the first volume of the Commons Journals ends, to 1909, when the new series of official reports of parliamentary debates begins, we are dependent for our knowledge of what was said in parliament almost entirely on private and unofficial reports. During the earlier part of this period these reports were based on notes taken surreptitiously, and were published in defiance or evasion of parliamentary orders. Afterwards each House, and especially the House of Commons, became less jealous of parliamentary reporters and tolerated their presence. Eventually parliament frankly and fully recognized the utility of publishing reports of parliamentary debates, gave every encouragement and facility to the preparation of these reports, and liberally subsidized, out of public money, a series of reports which, though not official, were authorized.

During the Long Parliament the House of Commons put every difficulty in the way of any reporting of its debates or proceedings. In special cases reports of particular speeches were printed by its order, but the printing of speeches without parliamentary authority was expressly prohibited and in some cases severely punished. This policy of prohibition continued until, and long after, the restoration of Charles II, and consequently our knowledge of parliamentary debates during this period is very scanty and fragmentary. For instance, of the debates during the first six years of Charles II's long 'Cavalier' Parliament, which met in 1661, there is no record whatever except a few references in letters, memoirs, and the like. In the closing years of the seventeenth century, and throughout the eighteenth century, the public demand for information about parliamentary proceedings grew rapidly and steadily, and had to be satisfied somehow. But the policy of prohibiting reports was maintained and enforced, and a severe contest was carried on between parliament and the press. This contest has been fully described in the pages of *May's Constitutional History*, and need not be repeated here. The two most important dates are 1738 and 1771. Before 1738 reports of debates appeared in such periodicals as the *London Magazine*, the *Gentleman's Magazine*, and the *Scots Magazine*. The names of the speakers were distinguished by initials, and, in order to escape the censure of parliament, the publication was postponed until the end of the session. In 1738 there was a great discussion in the House of Commons on the breach of privilege involved in these publications; the House prohibited the publication of debates on proceedings as well during the recess as during the sitting of parliament, and resolved to proceed with the utmost severity against offenders. The prohibitions were ineffectual and the struggle continued. The scene of debate was thinly veiled by the publisher under some such description as the senate of Great Lilliput, and the speakers were designated as Brutus or Mark Antony, or by other Roman titles. Meanwhile Woodgate and other prominent publishers were frequently being censured, committed to Newgate, or otherwise punished, by the indignant House. Stringent steps were taken for the exclusion of strangers, and the exclusion was so severely enforced during the parliament of 1768–74 that it has been sometimes called the unreported parliament. It was during this parliament that the great contest of 1771 occurred, when Colonel Onslow took the lead on behalf of privilege in the House of Commons, whilst Alderman Wilkes championed the printers, and ingeniously enlisted on their behalf the sympathies and authority of the City of London.

During this period of prohibition, how did the enterprising editors and publishers of magazines and other periodicals obtain the parliamentary information which, at much risk to themselves, they supplied to the public? This is a question on which Cave, the editor of the *Gentleman's Magazine*, and Samuel Johnson, the most famous of his contributors, have thrown some light. The publication of debates in the *Gentleman's Magazine* began in July 1732. In 1738, when Johnson was about thirty years old, he was employed by Cave to revise the notes and reports of Guthrie, his chief reporter, who was not a skilful writer. Soon, instead of correcting the reports, he drew them up himself, and eventually he wrote them all. From the sitting of 25 November 1740, to that of 22 November 1743, all the reports in the *Gentleman's Magazine* are from Johnson's hand, and, during that period, if we are to trust these reports, every parliamentary orator, without exception, when he rose to speak, delivered himself of a leading article in ample and sonorous Johnsonese. The reports were a great success; they sent up the circulation of the magazine, and were translated into French and other foreign languages.

About these reports Murphy, an early biographer of

Dr. Johnson, tells a curious story, which, though well known, will bear repetition. Some time in the later years of his life Johnson was dining with Foote, the actor. Among the company were Dr. Francis, known as the translator of Horace, and Murphy himself. An important debate towards the end of Sir Robert Walpole's administration being mentioned, Dr. Francis observed that Pitt's speech on that occasion was the best he had ever read. Many of the company remembered the debate, and some passages were cited with the approbation and applause of all present. During the ardour of conversation, Johnson remained silent. As soon as the warmth of praise subsided, he opened with these words, 'That speech I wrote in a garret in Exeter Street.' The company was struck with astonishment, and Francis asked for an explanation.

'Sir [said Johnson], I wrote it in Exeter Street. I never had been in the gallery of the House of Commons but once. Cave had interest with the doorkeepers. He, and the persons employed under him, gained admittance; they brought away the subject of discussion, the names of the speakers, the side they took, and the order in which they rose, together with notes of the arguments advanced in the course of the debate. The whole was afterwards communicated to me, and I composed the speeches in the form which they now have in the parliamentary debates.'

The company bestowed lavish encomiums on Johnson, and one of them praised his impartiality, observing that he dealt out reason and eloquence with an equal hand to both parties. 'That is not quite true', said Johnson. 'I saved appearances tolerably well, but I took care that the Whig dogs should not have the best of it.'

The account of this famous conversation was not

published until at least nineteen years after it was said to have taken place, and seems to contain some trifling inaccuracies, but, in the opinion of Dr. Birkbeck Hill, the highest authority on Johnson, 'the main facts may be true enough'.

In the struggle of 1771 the Commons were nominally victorious, but were practically defeated. Since that year the proceedings of both Houses of Parliament have been freely reported, but for a long time afterwards formidable difficulties stood in the way of anything like complete and accurate reports. There was no provision for the accommodation of reporters; strangers were admitted as a matter of favour and under inconvenient restrictions; they were apt to be regarded in the light of intruders into a London club, and their total exclusion was frequently and arbitrarily enforced under the orders of the House. Hence some of the most important debates and some of the most brilliant speeches of the eighteenth century have not been reported at all, whilst in other cases our knowledge of them is derived from scanty, imperfect, and, inaccurate notes. It was not until after the fire of 1834 that special provision was made for the accommodation of reporters, and it was not until 1888 that the rules for the admission and exclusion of 'strangers' were placed on a more rational footing. But it is needless to say that ever since the Reform Act of 1832, if not from an earlier date, the full and accurate reporting of parliamentary debates has been generally recognized as a matter of great public importance, and the provision of adequate accommodation and facilities for the public press has become one of the principal cares of the House.

At the present day those who wish to obtain information about the parliamentary debates of the past, would probably turn, in the first instance, for the earlier period, to the Parliamentary History, and for the later period to 'Hansard'. The compilation known as the Parliamentary History first appeared in 1751 and was then brought down to the date of the restoration of 1660. It was superseded and continued by Cobbett's well-known Parliamentary History, which came down to 1803. The materials used in this compilation are derived, partly from the rolls of parliament and the Journals of the two Houses, partly from authorized reports of individual peeches, partly from fragmentary, scattered, and unpublished sources, such as drafts or notes of speeches by members of parliament, but, for the eighteenth century, mainly from the accounts given in contemporary periodical publications such as those to which reference has been made above. When Cobbett's Parliamentary History was brought to a conclusion in 1803, it was succeeded by a series of reports which was at first known as Cobbett's Parliamentary Debates. In 1808 the printing of this series was taken over by Thomas C. Hansard, eldest son of the Luke Hansard who had been for many years, and was then, printer of the House of Commons Journals. The Hansards bought out the Cobbett interest in the publication, and after volume twenty-two (1822) the name of Cobbett disappeared from the title page. This is the publication which, in successive series, under different forms of management, and for years after the Hansard family had ceased to have any interest in it, was continued until the end of the year 1908, being known to all the world as Hansard. It superseded the various reports which had previously chronicled the debates of George III's reign, and succeeded in triumphing over various rivals such as the Mirror of Parliament

(1828–41). It was in its inception, and continued for many years to be, a purely private venture, supported by annual subscription from members of parliament and others, having no special reporters of its own, and deriving its materials from a collation of reports prepared for *The Times*, *Morning Chronicle*, and other leading newspapers, a collation which was often aided by the corrections of the speakers.

At the end of 1877, as the result of some discussion which had taken place in the House of Commons on the system of parliamentary reporting, an arrangement was made between the Chancellor of the Exchequer and the Mr. Hansard of the day under which, in consideration of Mr. Hansard undertaking to maintain a staff of special reporters, to report fully certain points which might be passed over by ordinary newspaper reporters as of little interest to their readers, and to limit the annual subscription to the series, the Treasury undertook to subsidize the publication from public money. Contracts of the same kind, but with varying terms, were renewed from time to time with Mr. Hansard and his successor, until the end of the year 1908.

But in that year the two Houses of Parliament, following the recommendations of a strong committee, determined to discontinue the system of subsidizing unofficial reports, and to appoint official reporters of their own. The new system came into operation at the beginning of the session of 1909, but the old name of 'Hansard' continued to be popularly applied to the published debates, and in 1944 it was formally adopted once more. Under present arrangements each House has its own staff of reporters, and its own separate reports. The reports of each day's debates in the Commons are distributed, in an unrevised form, by breakfast time next morning. The reports are made up to about 11 p.m. on the previous day, any reports of subsequent proceedings being reserved for the following number. The Lords were at first nervous about the form of their speeches, and did not allow them to be reported officially until opportunity had been given for their revision. The system has worked well, and it is a great convenience to members to have, in a handy form, official reports of each day's debates in time for use at the sitting of the following day. The reporting of debates in Standing Committees has been usual since 1919. With regard to private members' Bills a shorthand report is not printed unless the chairman, after consulting the minister concerned, thinks that the public interest demands it. The reporting of evidence given before Select Committees is customary.

In parliamentary language all persons who are not either members or officers of parliament are grouped together as strangers. In the days when reporting was an offence a reporter was a noxious variety of stranger who took notes which he had no business to take. Under the arrangements which have been made since, reporting has been recognized and encouraged and a distinction is drawn between reporters and visitors. In the House of Commons seats are reserved for reporters, both the official reporters and the representatives of newspapers, in the gallery at the Speaker's end of the House, and accommodation for their comfort and convenience is provided in adjoining rooms. The British Broadcasting Corporation is also allotted seats at the far end of the chamber facing the Speaker. By 'ancient privilege' claimed by successive holders of the office and hitherto continued by consent of the Serjeant-at-Arms, the

Remembrancer of the City of London has been allowed admission and a seat 'under the gallery'. The Official Gallery, better known as 'the box', behind the Speaker's chair and to his right side, is occupied exclusively by departmental officials; their presence is often convenient for consultation with a minister during debates on Bills in which he is interested.

As regards accommodation for visitors, while the House of Commons has been permitted, on the destruction of its own chamber, to use that of the House of Lords, the old arrangements for the galleries have been reproduced as far as possible. In the former House of Commons there were special galleries for ambassadors, foreign ministers, Dominions visitors, and 'distinguished strangers'. Down to the end of 1908 the Ladies' Gallery was the only place to which ladies were admitted; its accommodation was scanty and its occupants' vision was obscured by bars and lattices. There is now no discrimination against women as visitors; the Speaker's small gallery is reserved for ladies only. Constituents and others who hope for opportunities of attending a debate in the House of Commons must not expect that seats are easily obtained. The galleries offer severely limited accommodation; members seeking admission orders for friends and acquaintances must take the luck of the ballot or the turn of the alphabet. The lobbies are often crowded with would-be spectators, and at night there may be queues of enthusiasts waiting for a seat which someone more fortunate has vacated.

The history of the struggle between the House of Commons on the one hand and the public and the press on the other, is a history of the survival of outworn forms and obsolete claims. Parliaments of the seventeenth century claimed against Stuart kings the right of private deliberation. Parliaments of later date maintained the tradition of privacy long after the reason for secrecy had disappeared, and in the eighteenth century used against the press and the public the weapon of privilege which their predecessors had used against an interfering king. Even in the nineteenth century, when it had been generally recognized that publicity of debate is an essential feature of parliamentary government, that without it the elector cannot be enlightened and informed as to the course of public affairs and the responsibility of the representative to those whom he represents cannot be enforced—even then the House of Commons, while relaxing and indeed reversing its practice, declined to alter its rules, so that the sittings of the House were, and indeed still are, in theory private though in practice public. Until 1875 a single member of the House of Commons could insist on the withdrawal of strangers, including reporters (he can still do so if a majority of the House agrees), and until 1909 there was no official report of its debates.

During the war which began in 1914 the experiment was made of holding secret sittings, from which reporters were excluded. It was not considered wholly successful. A like course was followed during the war which began in 1939. The publication of any report or description of the proceedings of a secret session was prohibited by a Defence Regulation, but there was a saving for the official version published by the Speaker.

CHAPTER X

THE HOUSE OF LORDS

PARLIAMENT, AS has been seen, consists of two houses or chambers, the House of Lords and the House of Commons, and it is the House of Lords that is usually referred to as the second chamber.

The House of Lords is the oldest second chamber in the world. Of all second chambers it is the most numerous and the most hereditary in its character. And it has suffered less change in its constitution than any legislative chamber with an approximate tenure of life. It is the lineal descendant of the great council of the Plantagenet kings, before that council was reinforced by the addition of elected members. But, though its constitution has not been materially altered since those days, its numbers and composition have greatly changed.

There are now nearly 850 members of the House of Lords, including royal princes, archbishops, dukes, marquesses, earls, viscounts, bishops, barons, and nine judicial life peers. To the Model Parliament of 1295 were summoned two archbishops, eighteen bishops, about seventy abbots and other heads of religious houses, seven earls, and forty-one barons, less than 140 in all. At first there was room for doubt and for the exercise of discretion as to who should be summoned individually as greater barons, and who should be left to be represented with other lesser barons. But the line was gradually drawn, and the fact that an individual writ of summons had been sent to a particular baron began to give an hereditary right to his heirs. Dukes first made their appearance under Edward III, marquesses under his successor, and viscounts under Henry VI. From 1387 the practice grew up of creating a peerage by the more formal method of granting letters patent, and this practice superseded the earlier system under which the right to attend as a peer depended on a writ of summons having been issued to an ancestor and obeyed. Peerages by writ may, in default of direct male heirs, descend through the female line, though the female holder of such a peerage does not receive a writ of summons to the House of Lords; peerages by letters patent ordinarily descend to male heirs only. The number of abbots summoned rapidly dwindled, and they disappeared altogether after the Reformation. The number of bishops was increased at that time, but remained stationary for centuries afterwards. When it was again increased in the nineteenth century a provision was made that not all the bishops should have seats in the House of Lords. Only twenty-four bishops now sit there, besides the archbishops; a junior bishop has to wait unless he holds the see of Durham, Winchester, or London. The bishops, who wear their episcopal robes, have their own benches on the right of the throne, and no temporal peer may speak therefrom.

Two points may be specially noticed about the early House of Lords.

In the first place, it was a small body, very small in comparison with the present House of Lords, small in comparison with the contemporary House of Commons. Before the Tudors the number of temporal peers never exceeded fifty-five, rarely reached that number, and once fell as low as twenty-three. During the Tudor reigns the number of temporal peers seems to have fluctuated round fifty. The number was increased under the Stuarts, but it was not until the eighteenth century that the lavish creation of peers began. Of the existing peerages only a very small proportion are really ancient.

In the second place, the proportion of hereditary members of the House was formerly much smaller than it is at present. Before the Reformation the spiritual peers, who were summoned in virtue of their office, could usually command a majority.

The union with Scotland in 1707, and the union with Ireland in 1801, gave rise to another classification of peerages. There are peerages of England created before 1707, peerages of Great Britain created between 1707 and 1801, and peerages of the United Kingdom created since 1801. All these confer on their holders an hereditary right to sit in the House of Lords. But, besides these, there are peerages of Scotland and peerages of Ireland, and the holders of these peerages have no right to sit in the House of Lords, unless they either hold also, as many of them do, peerages of the other class, or have been elected as representative peers by their brother peers of Scotland or Ireland. The Irish peers have enjoyed advantages over their Scottish brethren. In the first place, if elected representative peers, they were elected for life, and not for a single parliament, like the Scottish peers. Then, if they were not elected, they were eligible for seats in the House of Commons, though not for Irish seats. Lord Palmerston was an Irish peer, but sat in the House of Commons. Lord Curzon was an Irish peer before he became a peer of the United Kingdom, and would have been eligible to a seat in the House of

Commons if he had not been elected as a representative Irish peer. But our sympathies with the disabilities of Scottish peers may be tempered by the reflection that their number is small and dwindling. The power to create peers of Scotland has ceased, and, while there are sixteen Scottish representative peers, there are now not more than fifteen Scottish peers who are without the right to seats in the House of Lords, either as representative peers or in right of some other peerage. As for the Irish representative peers, their full complement would be twenty-eight, but, since the Irish constitutional changes in 1922, no election has taken place, the abolition of the office of Lord Chancellor of Ireland having caused the electoral machinery to lapse. Consequently by 1947 there were only eight Irish representative peers; after their lifetime, this element in the House of Lords will cease to exist. The right to create Irish peerages still remains, but it has not been exercised since 1898.

A woman may become a member of the House of Commons or a minister of the Crown, but may not sit or vote in the House of Lords. In 1919 Parliament enacted that a person should not be disqualified by sex or marriage from the exercise of any public function. Nevertheless the Lords declared, in the case of Viscountess Rhondda in 1922, that a peeress of the United Kingdom in her own right is not entitled to receive a writ of summons to Parliament. The removal of sex disqualification in 1919, it seems, could not be imagined to have had so tremendous a result as to admit a woman to the House of Lords.

The House of Lords shares most of its functions with the House of Commons, but its judicial functions are peculiar to itself. The control of the House of Lords, by way of appeal, over the action of the English courts of common law may be traced back to the time when it was the king's Great Council. The control was subsequently extended to the courts of chancery or equity in England, and to the courts of Scotland and Ireland. But it has never been extended to the ecclesiastical courts, or to the courts in British dominions beyond the seas. In appeals from these courts its place is taken by the Judicial Committee of the Privy Council.

Although the judicial functions of the House of Lords are of great antiquity, the activity of their exercise, and the mode in which they have been exercised, have varied much. During the greater part of the fifteenth and sixteenth centuries they were practically dormant. During most of the eighteenth century they were exercised by the Lord Chancellor of the day, 'sitting in judicial solitude', as Erskine May says, 'with two mute, untrained lords in the background to represent the collective wisdom of the court'.

Lord Selborne's scheme for amalgamating the courts threatened the judicial powers of the House of Lords with extinction, for the Supreme Court which he called into being was intended to be supreme in fact as well as in name, and its decisions were intended to be final. But before his Judicature Act came into operation it was amended by an Act of 1876 which restored the appellate jurisdiction of the House of Lords and provided for its exercise by salaried lords of appeal in ordinary. These lords of appeal were intended to be official peers and to hold their peerages only during their tenure of office, for the decision in the Wensleydale case that the grant of a peerage for life would not entitle the grantee to a seat in the House of Lords was then still fresh in men's memories, and it was deemed expedient to draw a distinction between official peerages and life peerages. But eleven years afterwards this distinction was removed, and an Act of 1887 enabled retiring lords of appeal to retain their peerages during their life.

The Act of 1876 provides that no appeal can be heard by the House of Lords unless at least three persons with specified legal qualifications are present. But the judgement is still, technically, the judgement of the House of Lords; the Act does not disqualify any member of that House for the exercise of judicial functions; and any peer, however unlearned, may, in theory, attend and take an active part in the proceedings of an appeal. What would be the result of his attempting to do so is another question. The position is interesting, because it illustrates the possibility of the House of Lords delegating its functions, without any express change in the law, to a specially qualified committee, and also illustrates the large part played by legal fiction in our constitutional arrangements. The judicial functions of the House of Lords are performed by approximately a dozen trained lawyers, and the other members of the House take no part in and share no responsibility for these proceedings. Judgement is delivered in the form of speeches to the House by the lords composing the court.

Besides its appellate functions the House of Lords has original jurisdiction of three kinds, namely in impeachments, trial of peers, and peerage claims. An impeachment may be brought by the House of Commons, acting as prosecutor, against any person for 'high crimes and misdemeanours.' The Commons send to the Lords articles of impeachment, to which the accused is directed to deliver replies; to these again the Commons may formulate 'replications'. The trial then takes place in the House of Lords, after which the Lords, as judges, return their verdict. The last impeachment, brought against Lord Melville for malversation, took place in 1806.

It is the privilege of peers or peeresses charged with felony or treason that they are not to be tried for these offences save by their peers. The Lord High Steward, who is appointed for the occasion, presides, and the peers present, who are robed, usually require the attendance of the judges in order to invite their opinion on any point of law before the verdict is declared. Not long after a trial of this kind had occurred in 1935, a Bill to abolish this ancient jurisdiction was passed by the House of Lords, but it had no opportunity to make further progress in the Commons.

Peerage claims are referred to the House of Lords by the Crown and are dealt with by the Lords' Committee of Privileges before whom counsel may be heard.

The arrangements during a judicial sitting of the lords are quite different from those during a sitting for purposes of legislation or debate. Judicial business begins in the morning, and ends before the ordinary afternoon business begins. Technically, there is only one sitting, in two parts, with an interval between them. The sitting is ushered in by prayers, usually read by one of the bishops. The Lord Chancellor sits at a table in front of the bar; the other members of the court sit at desks placed on either side of him.

Although the judicial business is thus conducted as part of an ordinary sitting of the House, it can proceed (by virtue of a statute of 1876) while parliament is prorogued. The arrangements when parliament is dissolved are slightly different; the law lords may then be authorized under the sign manual to sit 'in the name of the House of Lords'. They thus sat after the dissolution in 1945; their proceedings were preceded by prayers (read by a law lord), but the mace was not brought in, and the Lord Chancellor wore neither wig nor robes.

The general business of the House of Lords occupies some three or four hours in the afternoon. Sittings rarely extend beyond the dinner hour. The amount of business to be transacted is much less than in the House of Commons; questions are few; there are no estimates to discuss, and debates on the different stages of Bills are, as a rule, much shorter. Consequently it has not been found necessary to adopt any precise allocation of time, or to have recourse to any of the methods for shortening proceedings with which the House of Commons is familiar. Rules are few and procedure is elastic. All business is placed on the order paper in the order in which it is received; no difference is made between Government and private members' business; if, however, the paper becomes congested and it seems likely that the legislative programme of the Government may be jeopardized, precedence is given (by the suspension of a Standing Order) to Government business.

Except when the House is in committee, the Lord Chancellor, as Speaker of the House, occupies the woolsack. But, as already mentioned, his position differs from that of the Speaker of the House of Commons. He has no power to make authoritative rulings on points of order; such matters are decided by the peers themselves who, subject to their Standing Orders, are masters of their own procedure and take pride in keeping it flexible. The Lord Chancellor does not call by name upon the next speaker to address the House in debate; if two lords rise together and neither appears disposed to give way, the House calls for the speaker whom it desires to hear. When the Lord Chancellor takes part in a debate, he steps a few paces aside from the woolsack, speaking from his place as a peer. Sometimes, however, a Lord Chancellor has presided over the chamber without being a peer. He has no casting vote. If on a division the votes cast are equal, the issue is decided in accordance with 'the ancient rule' *semper praesumitur pro negante*, on the principle that a majority is required before a change is made.

Subject to the important exception of financial measures, almost any Public Bill may be introduced in either House. But in modern practice the more important Bills are, as a rule, introduced in the House of Commons, with the result that in the early part of the session there is a dearth of legislative business in the House of Lords whilst at the end there is much congestion, and Bills brought from the other House are hurried through with what is sometimes described as indecent and unseemly haste. Complaints have often been made on that score, and it has been suggested that parliamentary time might be saved if more of the important Bills were introduced in the House of Lords in the early part of the session, when the other House is necessarily much engaged with financial business. But the Government of the day, whichever party is in power, does not show much inclination to adopt this suggestion. The minister responsible for the Bill may be a member of the House of Commons, and may wish to launch it himself. Further it is felt that, until a measure has been discussed in the popular House, it is difficult to ascertain the trend and force of public opinion, what chance the measure has of becoming law, and what amendments it is likely to require in deference to hostile or friendly criticism. But the practice is not invariable; some important measures, such as the Road Traffic Act 1930 which inaugurated the Highway Code, have been introduced in the House of Lords.

It is the strict limitation of powers for dealing with finance that constitutes the main difference between the work of the House of Lords and the work of the House of Commons, and that is at the root of the comparatively subordinate position occupied in the modern constitution by the former House. The earlier stages in the development of the principle that grants of money must be initiated in the House of Commons have been described in our first chapter. To the recognition of the principle by Henry IV in 1407 much importance is attached by constitutional historians, but it was not until some centuries afterwards, not until after the Restoration of 1660, when the two Houses resumed those normal functions which had been interrupted by the revolution and the Cromwellian interregnum, that the House of Commons formally and distinctly asserted, as against the other House, their exclusive right to control taxation. In 1671 they resolved 'that in all aids given to the king by the Commons, the rate or tax ought not to be altered by the Lords'. In 1678 they again resolved, in fuller language,

'that all aids and supplies, and aids to His Majesty in parliament, are the sole gift of the Commons; and all Bills for the granting of any such aids or supplies ought to begin with the Commons; and that it is the undoubted and sole right of the Commons to direct, limit and appoint in such Bills the ends, purposes, considerations, conditions, limitations and qualifications of such grants, which ought not to be changed or altered by the House of Lords.'

The resolutions of 1671 and 1678 were emphasized and expanded by a famous resolution passed by the House of Commons on the 6th of July, 1860, at the time of the quarrel between the two Houses over the repeal of the paper duty, and it is upon these resolutions that is based the practice of the House of Commons in dealing with cases where they conceive that their financial rights or privileges have been infringed by the other House.

The main rules on the observance of which the Commons insist may be formulated as follows—

1. The Lords ought not to initiate any legislative proposal embodied in a public Bill and imposing a charge on the people, whether by way of taxes, rates, or otherwise, or regulating the administration or application of money raised by such a charge.

2. The Lords ought not to amend any such legislative proposal by altering the amount of a charge, or its incidence, duration, mode of assessment, levy or collection, or the administration or application of money raised by such a charge.

It must be observed that these are claims by the House of Commons, claims which have not been formally admitted by the other House, and which have not taken the form of rules embodied in any law or Standing Order binding on that House. But they have been recognized and relied on by leading members of the House of Lords, on both sides of the House, have been generally observed in the practice of both Houses, and, so far as constitutional law depends on usage and practice, may be treated as forming part of the constitutional law of the country.

It must be further observed that the application of these general rules to particular cases may and often does give rise to questions of difficulty and complexity, and that to insist too strictly on adherence to them would often cause much practical inconvenience. What is a 'charge on the people'? How far ought one to pursue possible consequences and results in considering whether such a charge or burden is imposed? What is exactly meant by the administration or application of money raised by a charge? All administration involves, or may involve, expenditure of public money, and would not a too literal interpretation of these words hamper the legislative action of the House of Lords in a way which is neither intended nor desirable? Questions of this kind have frequently been raised for the consideration both of the Speaker and of the House of Commons, and, as a rule, have been settled in accordance with the dictates of common sense and general convenience, but in such a way as to leave the procedure elastic and the rulings not always easy to reconcile with each other. In the case of Private Bills, the Commons have expressly waived some of their privileges by Standing Order. In the case of Public Bills the Commons would not receive from the Lords a Bill whose sole purpose was to impose a charge, but, when the financial provisions are merely incidental to the main objects of the Bill, these provisions are, by a convention, omitted by the Lords before the Bill is sent to the Commons where they are reinserted. When the Lords make amendments to Bills sent to them from the

Commons, the Speaker looks to see whether any of the amendments affect the privileges of the Commons and informs that House accordingly. If the Commons desire to accept any of these, they waive their privilege, saving their position by having a special entry made in their Journals explaining their reasons for acceptance. If they decide to reject the amendments, they usually send a message, giving some general reason, such as that the amendment would interfere with the public revenue, and adding that 'the Commons consider that it is unnecessary on their part to offer any further reason, hoping the above reason may be deemed sufficient'. This is the conventional form of hinting at a claim of 'privilege', and the hint is in most cases accepted by the Lords on the very sound principle that it is not worth while to raise a big question except on a big issue. The practice of both Houses has been, as a rule, conciliatory, and, though questions of privilege between the two Houses have occasionally roused grumblings of discontent, they have very rarely caused a serious breach.

The rejection of the Finance Bill in 1909 was, of course, an exception. The constitutional arguments on either side are well known. On the one side it was argued that this particular Bill was something different from and more than an ordinary 'finance' or money Bill, and that, even if its scope had been merely financial, the right of the House of Lords to reject a 'money Bill', though rarely exercised, existed, was substantial, and had never been denied. On the other hand it was argued that the alteration of practice made by Gladstone in 1861, when he embodied all the financial proposals of the year in a single measure, had merely affirmed and strengthened the true constitutional relations between the two Houses, and that the rejection of a Finance Bill was as inconsistent with sound constitutional practice as its amendment. The relations between the two Houses are not governed by statute and are beyond the cognizance of the courts of law. Therefore of legal rights and powers in the narrower sense there is no question. The question is one of constitutional usage and propriety.

But, if there is a debatable borderland between the rights and privileges claimed by the Commons, and those admitted by the House of Lords, the fact remains that the fiscal powers of the latter House, the powers of the Lords with respect to revenue, expenditure, and taxation, are strictly circumscribed. They are not consulted about the estimates, about the amounts of money to be raised, or the purposes to which those amounts are to be appropriated. Proposals for taxation do not reach them until these proposals have been sanctioned by the other House, and then in a form which makes criticism difficult. And, as the power of the executive government depends on the power of the purse, the whole range of executive government is placed beyond their effective control. They can criticize, and their criticisms are often valuable and influential, but they cannot enforce their criticisms. The ministry cannot afford to disregard a resolution or vote of the House of Commons expressing or implying condemnation of their policy or action. Such a resolution or vote must shake them, may destroy them. But they can afford to disregard a condemnatory resolution passed by the Lords. In short, it is to the Commons, and not to the Lords, that the executive government is responsible, so far as responsibility implies enforceable control. What then remains to the House of Lords? Very great powers. In the sphere of executive government, the Lords can, and do, express their opinion with greater freedom than is possible in a body where the bonds of party discipline are more strictly drawn; and those who take part in and influence their debates speak with all the authority that attaches to high position, to recognized ability, and to ripe experience. Such authority is not to be measured by votes on a division, any more than the influence of debates in the House of Commons is to be so measured; it is operative although it cannot be enforced. Debates in the House of Lords on questions of policy and administration are often of great value, carry great weight, and materially influence the opinion of the country and the action of the Government.

In the sphere of legislation, subject to the fiscal limitations referred to above, to some minor technical differences, and, now, to the provisions of the Parliament Act, the powers of the two Houses are co-equal and concurrent. Inasmuch, however, as the more important and controversial Bills are usually introduced in the House of Commons, the legislative functions of the Lords are, in these cases, the exercise of powers of revision and of powers of rejection.

The need of revision after a legislative measure has passed through the rough-and-tumble of a popular assembly is recognized on all sides, and the utility of the revision exercised in the House of Lords is generally admitted. If, for instance, the progress of a Bill through the House of Commons has been subject to a time-table, there may be clauses which received little attention. Moreover, the Speaker's power of selecting the amendments for discussion in the Commons, while it concentrates debate upon the most material and significant of them, may seem to exclude proposals for the improvement of a Bill in detail. Be that as it may, observers do not always realize that, though the Lords often exercise advantageously independent powers of criticism, yet a large number, probably the majority, of the amendments made in Public Bills after they have passed from the Commons to the Lords are suggested by the promoters of the Bill, and are made, either in pursuance of pledges for further consideration given in the former House, or to remove inaccuracies, obscurities, inconsistencies, or other defects of form which had been discovered, but for the removal of which time or opportunity had failed in the initiating House. In such cases the House of Lords might be considered rather an instrument than an organ of revision.

The power of amending a Bill may be so exercised as to extend beyond revision of form and details, and to make such alterations as are, in the opinion of the promoters, inconsistent with the fundamental principles of the measure. Where the power is so exercised, the action of the House of Lords is tantamount to rejection.

How far, and under what conditions, is it expedient or consistent with modern constitutional practice that the Lords should exercise their power of rejecting a Bill sent from the Commons, of delaying its passage, or of fundamentally altering its provisions? And if differences arise on these points between the two Houses, how should they be determined? To state these problems is to raise questions which are of the greatest magnitude and difficulty, and which led in 1909 to one of the sharpest constitutional conflicts of modern times.

When parliament was reconstituted after the restoration of Charles II, questions were speedily raised about the relations between the powers and jurisdiction of the two Houses. And, at a somewhat later date, at times when the political complexion of the majority in the Lords was Whig and Broad Church, whilst that of the Commons was Tory and High Church, the differences of opinion between the two Houses were sometimes serious. But, during the greater part of the eighteenth century, and indeed down to the time of the Reform Act of 1832, there were no serious conflicts between them Nor was there any reason why there should be. The causes and elements of difference were absent. The members of the House of Commons were, in the main, drawn from the same classes as the members of the House of Lords, represented the same opinions and interests, and were, in many cases, directly nominated by individual peers. Since 1832 the position has been materially altered. The extension of the franchise, the advance of democratic ideas, and the change of views about the powers and duties of the State in dealing with social and economic problems, have tended, and are daily tending, to widen the gulf between the popular House and the House which has specially represented tradition, aristocracy, and wealth. The Lords have, for several generations, met the difficulties of the position by prudently and sagaciously limiting the exercise of their powers. They no longer claim the right—the constitutional as distinguished from the legal right—to exercise concurrent powers of legislation. When a Bill is sent from the Commons, the Lords do not, in practice, exercise freely either the right to reject it if it is not in accordance with their own views, or the right to make substantial alterations. What they claim, according to an authoritative exposition by a leading member of their House, is the right and duty 'to arrest the progress of such measures whenever we believe that they have been insufficiently considered and that they are not in accord with the deliberate judgement of the country'. In short, the claim made by them is to act as arbiters between the Commons and the country. The constitutional position thus assumed would be stronger if the questions at issue were questions of fact or law, the decision of which could be delegated to legal experts and dealt with in a strictly judicial spirit. As it is, the Lords are open to the charge of being actuated by political or economic motives, and the need of devising some better method of reconciling and adjusting differences between the two branches of the legislature has been recognized on all sides. From the Conservative point of view there are sound and solid arguments for a House of Lords, but it would appear to many that to defend an aristocratic institution with democratic arguments is neither easy nor safe. Proposals for reforming the House have naturally been concerned to reduce the number of peers qualified to sit (as in the Bill tentatively initiated by Lord Salisbury in 1933) or to add or substitute a scheme of recruitment to dilute or replace the hereditary principle (as in Lord Rosebery's plan of 1888 or the Bryce Conference recommendations of thirty years later). If a reformed House of Lords means a strengthened House of Lords, what prospect is there of reform?

In the seventeenth century conferences between the two Houses were of frequent occurrence. They were by no means confined to differences between the Houses, but extended to such subjects as the proposed union with Scotland, the general affairs of Scotland and Ireland, the Petition of Right and the Bill of Rights, the Army Plot of one year and the Popish Plot of another, and, finally, the impeachment of great men. In fact they ranged over the whole field of parliamentary affairs. The tendency of the eighteenth century was to limit their number and scope, and to give them a more formal character. They were usually, but not exclusively, confined to cases of differences of opinion about amendments made by one House in Bills coming from the other, for it had become a rule of practice that, while agreement with any such amendment might be signified by message, disagreement involved a conference. These conferences were conducted by 'managers' appointed by each House, the etiquette was very strict, and the proceedings were very formal. The Lords sat with their hats on their heads; the members of the Commons stood bareheaded. One of the managers from the House which initiated the conference read out the reasons for disagreement, and delivered the paper on which they were written to one of the managers of the other House. Then the managers parted and each set of managers reported the proceedings to the House from which they came. That was all. These formal conferences were sometimes supplemented by what were called 'free conferences', affording opportunity for discussion. But the free conferences became formal and useless, and the practice of holding them was finally abandoned in 1740, with a single subsequent exception. This exception was in 1836, when an abortive attempt was made to settle, by means of a free conference, a difference between the two Houses over a municipal reform Bill. The practice of holding formal conferences survived longer, and one of them, on the resolutions preliminary to the introduction of the great measure of 1833 for amending the charters of the East India Company, is described by Macaulay in a letter to his sister (17 June 1833).

'To-day we took up our resolutions about India to the House of Lords. The two Houses held a conference on the subject in an old Gothic room called the Painted Chamber. The painting consists of a mildewed daub of a woman in the niche of one of the windows. The Lords sat in little cocked hats along a table; and we stood uncovered on the other side and delivered in our resolutions. I thought that before long it may be our turn to sit, and theirs to stand.'

These conferences involved, among other inconveniences, a temporary suspension of the business of both Houses. At last it occurred to some sensible person that the reasons for a disagreement might as well be signified by message as at a conference, and accordingly, by resolutions of both Houses agreed to at conferences held in May 1851, messages were substituted for conferences unless a conference was preferred. The change was permissive only; the old procedure by conferences has never been finally abolished, and it would still be open to any member of the House, with an antiquarian turn of mind, to move that it should be revived. But such a motion is not likely to be made. What happens in the present day, when there is a disagreement over amendments in a Bill, is that private and informal conferences take place between prominent members of both parties in the case of an important Government Bill, or between the promoters and opponents or critics of a Bill in the case of other measures, and attempts are made to arrive at some compromise. If the attempts are unsuccessful, the Bill drops and fails to become law, for, unless the Parliament Act is brought into play, concurrence of both Houses is needed before a Bill can be submitted for the king's assent.

Messages still frequently pass from one House to the other, and mainly relate to Bills, conveying information as to what either House has done on a Bill or wishes the other to do. In former times these messages used to be brought from the Lords by Masters in Chancery, legal functionaries with large emoluments and small duties, who were abolished in the last century. Messages from the Commons were brought up by the members themselves, and in 1831 and 1832 Lord John Russell brought his Reform Bills in his own hands to the bar of the House of Lords. At the present day these messages are brought from each House by the Clerk of the House, who may be seen occasionally attending for this purpose in his wig and gown at the bar of the other House.

The rejection of the Finance Bill in 1909, following, as it did, the rejection of other important Government measures, brought the differences between the two Houses to a crisis. A general election ensued, and maintained Mr. Asquith's government in power, though with a reduced majority. The Finance Bill of the year was reintroduced in the new parliament and became law. The Government moved and carried three resolutions for restricting the legislative powers of the House of Lords, and for shortening the duration of parliament. These resolutions were based on, but differed in some respects from, a resolution passed by the House of Commons at the instance of Sir Henry Campbell Bannerman in June 1907. A Bill founded on these resolutions was introduced, but further proceedings on it were stayed by the death of King Edward VII. A conference on the subject was then held between eight members of the two

Houses, four from each political party, and this conference was still sitting when parliament adjourned for an autumn recess. When parliament reassembled in November 1910, it was announced that the conference had failed to arrive at an agreement. Some important debates took place in the House of Lords, and that House passed resolutions of a general character for reforming their constitution and for regulating the relations between the two Houses.

The short parliament of 1910 was dissolved at the end of November, and the general election of December gave the Government a majority practically identical with that with which they went to the country. The Parliament Bill was re-introduced at the beginning of the session of 1911, and became law in August 1911, after some eventful scenes. The Lords had made amendments to which the Commons refused to agree, and the resistance of the Lords was only overcome by an authoritative intimation that the king had been advised by his ministers, and had consented, to create a number of peers sufficient to meet the exigencies of the case. Even then the motion not to insist on the amendments was carried only by 131 to 114.

The main provisions of the Parliament Act are these:

1. If the Lords withhold their assent to a money Bill for more than one month after the Bill has reached them, the Bill may be presented for the king's assent, and, on that assent being given, will become law without the consent of the Lords. The Act gives a definition of a 'money Bill', and it is for the Speaker of the House of Commons to certify that a Bill falls within the definition. Before giving his certificate he is to consult two members of the House of Commons appointed for that purpose.

2. If a Bill other than a money Bill is passed by the Commons in three successive sessions, whether of the same parliament or not, it may, on a third rejection by the Lords, be presented for the king's assent, and, on that assent being given, will become law. But two years must elapse between the date of the second reading in the first of those sessions and the date at which the Bill passes the Commons a third time.[1]

3. Five years (as mentioned earlier) is substituted for seven years as the maximum duration of a parliament.

How, it may be asked, have these provisions worked in the period since 1911?

The first of them in effect created a new category of financial Bill. Besides the ordinary Supply Bill in respect of which the Commons claimed certain privileges expressly preserved by the Parliament Act, there is now the Money Bill certified by the Speaker as coming within the definition prescribed by that Act. There have been some half-dozen of such Bills annually. In two cases the Lords amended the Bill and the Commons accepted the amendment. In one case (the Safeguarding of Industries Bill in 1919) the Commons rejected amendments made by the Lords but preferred to rely on their ancient privileges rather than present the Bill for royal assent under the Parliament Act. During the period from 1911 to 1945 there were no fewer than twenty Finance Bills which the Speaker did not certify as coming within the statutory definition.

As regards the second provision, only two Bills have received the royal assent thereunder after having been

[1] This chapter was written before the introduction in November 1947 of the Bill to reduce the two-year period to one year.

three times rejected by the Lords, namely the Bills which became the Government of Ireland Act and the Welsh Church Act in 1914. After the outbreak of war in that year both these Acts were by statute suspended. The former was repealed in 1920 without having operated. The disestablishment of the Church in Wales under the latter took effect in 1920.

The third provision (the five-year limit to the life of a Parliament) is, of course, no more permanent or final than any other enactment. The Parliament which was elected in 1935 did not terminate in 1940, but was prolonged, as we have seen, by a series of continuing statutes year by year till 1945.

After the general election of 1945 the new House of Commons contained a substantial majority of supporters of the Labour party. The pace at which its voluminous legislation was taken emphasized the usefulness of a second chamber which is content to revise Bills without wrecking them. The Lords amended the Labour Government's Bills; the Commons agreed or disagreed with the Lords' amendments or suggested other amendments in lieu thereof. In the Transport Bill of 1947, for instance, the Lords inserted 210 amendments. The Commons accepted 173 of these; as the Lords did not 'insist' upon the remainder, no constitutional crisis arose. If a serious clash occurred between the two Houses, the Parliament Act exists to end it. Slow as its machinery may be, it is a much less clumsy expedient than the traditional remedy (invoked by way of threat in certain historic crises) whereby the Prime Minister advises the Crown to create new peers in such numbers and of such sympathies as will overcome any resistance.

CHAPTER XI

COMPARATIVE

John Bright's phrase that 'England is the mother of parliaments' has become so hackneyed that one is almost ashamed to repeat it. But it expresses an important historical truth. It is a fact that the constitution and procedure of the legislature in every other country, with the possible exception of the constitutional features which survived so long in Hungary, have been copied directly or indirectly from, or at least based on, ideas suggested by, the English model.

The first of these copyists were, as was proper and natural, men who were our own kith and kin, the framers of the constitution of the United States. And it is specially instructive to compare the ways of the British parliament with the ways of the American Congress, because the comparison shows how a people starting with the same habits, traditions, and modes of thought as our own, may, by making a cardinal point of a different constitutional principle, the severance of executive and legislative authority, arrive at curiously different results.

The delegates who met in convention at Philadelphia in 1787, under the presidency of George Washington, and with Alexander Hamilton as their master spirit, to devise a form of common government for the thirteen American States who had obtained their independence, naturally looked, in the first instance, for guidance and suggestion, to the forms of government then existing in their own States.

The constitutions of these States had been developed out of charters granted to them by the king when they were English colonies, and differed in various particulars. But they all had two features in common.

In each of them there was a governor and a legislature; and the governor, who was at the head of the executive power, was independent of, and not responsible to, the legislature. In none of them was the executive government conducted by ministers who were members of and responsible to the legislature. In none of them was there a system of Cabinet government, or parliamentary government, such as exists at the present day in the United Kingdom and in the British self-governing Dominions beyond the seas. And, if we ask why parliamentary or Cabinet government has not taken root in the United States, whilst it has taken root in the British self-governing Dominions, perhaps the chief reason is historical, namely, that the constitution of the old American colonies, of the States which succeeded them, and of the federal government which held these States together, was suggested by and resembled the English constitution before the Cabinet system had grown up or its principles were understood, whilst the constitutions of the modern British self-governing Dominions are modelled on the existing constitution of the United Kingdom.

The separation of the executive from the legislature was thus one of the common features in the constitutions of the American States at the time of their union. Another was that in almost all of them the legislature then consisted (as, except in Nebraska, it still consists) of two houses. The need for two chambers has since then been exalted into an axiom of political science, and may at least claim to be a political dogma which has obtained very general acceptance. But, according to Bryce, the origin of the two-chamber system in America is to be sought rather in history than in theory, and is due, partly to the previous existence in some colonies of a small governor's council in addition to the popular representative body, partly to a natural disposition to imitate the mother country, with its Lords and Commons.

These, then, were the models which the framers of the United States constitution had before them, State constitutions with the executive independent of the legislature, and with the legislature divided into two houses or chambers. And in adopting these two features they were influenced, not only by the natural tendency to imitation, but also by general considerations and practical needs. Among the political ideas which were 'in the air' in the eighteenth century there was none that exercised greater influence on the American mind than the doctrine of the separation of powers. This doctrine owed its popularity to Montesquieu, who had based it on a generalization, a hasty and imperfect generalization, from certain features of the British constitution. According to this doctrine the legislative, executive, and judicial functions of the State ought to be separate from and independent of each other. There ought to be separate organs for each, working together, but none of them dependent on the other. The men who met at Philadelphia found some support for this doctrine in the existing constitutions of their own States; it was consonant with their views as to the expediency of guarding against the risk of concentrating powers in a single man or set of men; they adopted it as a cardinal principle of their new constitution. They were naturally disposed also to divide their legislature into two houses as the legislatures in most of their States were divided. And they found in this division a solution of the greatest practical difficulty which they had to encounter, that of reconciling the demand for a common government with the demand of the smaller States for recognition and safeguarding of their separate rights. Under the constitution which they devised, the House of Representatives was to represent the nation on the basis of population, whilst the Senate was to represent the States. There were to be, and are, two senators from each State, small or large, but the representatives in the other House were to be, and are, distributed among the States in proportion to population, so that the more populous States outweigh the others.

Thus came into being the President, representing the executive power, the two Houses of Congress, representing the legislative power, and the Supreme Court, representing the judicial power, each authority independent within its own sphere.

Suppose a visitor from England, familiar with the working of parliamentary government at Westminster, were to arrive at Washington at the beginning of a new session, what resemblances and differences would be likely to strike him?

The first thing that would probably strike him in both houses of the legislature would be the absence of anything corresponding to the Treasury or Government Bench. Under the constitution no person holding any office under the United States can be a member of either House of Congress during his continuance in office. Consequently, neither the President, nor his Cabinet, the ministers who are at the head of his executive departments, can sit in either House. In England the ministers who are responsible for the executive work of government are members of one of the two Houses of the legislature; they are responsible for their actions to parliament, and in particular to the House of Commons; and, in turn, they can, as leaders of the dominant party, influence and control the action of that House.

In the United States the President does not enjoy the immunity from responsibility for political and administrative action which attaches to the English king, but he has more power: he not only reigns, but governs. He and his ministers have not to answer for their actions to Congress as the king's ministers have to answer for their actions to parliament; but, on the other hand, they cannot, like English ministers, guide and control the action of the legislature.

By another article of the constitution the President is required to recommend to the consideration of Congress such measures as he shall judge necessary and expedient. He does so by a message to Congress at the beginning of the session, and thus his message bears some resemblance to the King's Speech at the opening of parliament. But what a difference! The King's Speech is prepared by the king's ministers, and contains a programme of their legislative policy. This programme they are in a position to carry out, so far as time and circumstances permit, with the aid of their party, and for any failure to carry it out they will be called to account. But the President has no ministers to represent him in Congress, or to give effect to his wishes and intentions about legislation. His message is duly read, is duly referred, without debate, to the appropriate committee, and nothing more need be heard of it.

The English visitor would probably note in the procedure of Congress sundry forms and usages which will remind him of Westminster. This is not surprising. Thomas Jefferson, when Vice-President of the United States, and therefore President of the Senate, compiled, for the use of the Senate, a manual of procedure based on the practice, rulings, and precedents of the English parliament. Jefferson's manual is still authoritative for the procedure of both Houses of Congress.

But if the visitor attends the sittings of Congress, especially of the larger and more popular house, the House of Representatives, which corresponds in some measure to the House of Commons, he will note differences greater than the resemblances.

There is not so much debating. The room of assembly is larger than the House of Commons at Westminster, and the accommodation for members is ampler and more convenient. But the acoustic qualities have been inferior. It has been difficult for a member to make himself heard, and easy debate in a conversational tone has been impossible. That is one reason. Other reasons are, that the less formal sittings of the House, which in England are called committees of the whole House and in the United States committees of the whole, are less frequent at Washington than at Westminster, and that at Washington both the first and the second reading of Bills are formal stages, and every Bill goes to some one of the numerous committees of the House, and from these committees most Bills never emerge. It is in these committees that is done the bulk of the legislative business of Congress, including the financial business done at Westminster in Committee of Supply and in the proceedings on the Budget. Congressional government is government by committees of Congress.

The visitor to Washington might have the curiosity to look at the list of the Bills introduced into Congress, and to examine some of them, and see how they compare with Bills introduced at Westminster. Here again he would find startling differences. The total number of Bills, Public and Private, introduced in a single session of parliament has in normal times been counted by hundreds. In the sixtieth Congress at Washington, that is to say in the years 1909 and 1910, he might discover that as many as 44,500 Bills and resolutions were introduced. By resolutions are meant legislative proposals, not technically in the form of Bills. Of all these Bills and legislative proposals only about 275 became law—the remainder found a burial-place in the committees to which they were consigned. Thus the total output of legislation did not differ much from that of an average British session, but the proportion between Bills introduced and Bills passed differed enormously. In more recent years, though the statistics fluctuate violently, Washington seems to entertain far fewer Bills and to produce far more statutes. For the 75th Congress (to take the pre-war years 1939 and 1940) the figures show that 1,759 out of a total of 10,940 Bills became law.

In American legislation the British distinction between Government Bills and private members' Bills is, of course, absent, for the executive government is not represented in the House by any of its members. If the President, or if any of his ministers, wishes to have a particular Bill introduced, he must apply to some unofficial member of Congress, and the Bill, when introduced, will take its chance with other Bills.

Nor is there any distinction between Public and Private Bills. The great majority of the Bills introduced have dealt with local and personal questions and would have been classed in England as Private Bills. Very many of them have dealt with some single matter such as the grant of a pension to a particular person or the frontage of a particular building. They have been suggested by and designed to meet some individual case, not to effect any general change in the law. Many of them also deal with matters which in Britain would be left to departmental orders and regulations. Where, as in the United States, a line is drawn between the region of legislation and the region of executive government, the legislature is often to be found crossing the boundary and poaching on its neighbour's preserves. In Congress, ministers cannot be jogged to action by questions and motions.

In the Parliament at Westminster, as has been seen, the Ministry are mainly responsible for arranging the business, and distributing the time of the House of Commons. They thus act as a business committee of the House. In the House of Representatives there is no such committee, but the Speaker to some extent takes its place, and wields powers which place him in an entirely different position from the Speaker of the House of Commons. All the business of the House is distributed among, and mainly transacted in, about a score (before 1947 there were some fifty) of standing committees appointed at the beginning of the session, and it is the Speaker who nominates the members of these committees, and also appoints their chairman. Among these committees are the committees of ways and means and of appropriations, which regulate the taxation and expenditure of the Federal government, and the rules committee, which determines whether special facilities should be given for the consideration of such Bills as succeed in emerging from the committees to which they have been referred. Without such facilities no important Bills could pass, and the facilities granted often include stringent limitations of time and speech, more stringent than those imposed by the English 'closure' or 'guillotine'. The constitution of these committees is the first piece of work which the Speaker has to undertake after his appointment, and probably the most difficult and anxious work which he has to perform, for on the way in which it is performed depends the course of business in the session. Thus the American Speaker is not, like his prototype at Westminster, an impartial and judicial presiding authority, but a powerful party leader.

Last, but not least, among the differences between Parliament and Congress may be noted the fact that Parliament is supreme and uncontrolled in the exercise of its legislative powers, unfettered by a written constitution or by membership of a federal community. To use the language of an authoritative writer,

'Parliament is a sovereign and constituent assembly. It can make and unmake any and every law, change the form of government and the succession to the Crown, interfere with the course of justice, extinguish the most sacred private rights of the citizen. Between it and the people at large there is no legal distinction, because the whole plenitude of the people's rights and powers resides in it. Both practically and legally it is the only and the supreme depositary of the authority of the nation, and is therefore, within the sphere of law, irresponsible and omnipotent.'

Such are some of the resemblances and differences, of which the most complete and masterly exposition is to be found in Bryce's *American Commonwealth.* They will suffice to show how widely the characteristics of the American legislature have diverged from those of the venerable body which may fairly claim to be its parent stock.

We may pass to the continent of Europe. When the Napoleonic deluge subsided in the early part of the nineteenth century, it left all the European governments shattered and in ruins. The constitution of the United Kingdom alone remained standing and apparently unshaken, and it was to England that statesmen looked for their model when they set about to repair old or build new constitutions. Hence came the legislative bodies, each with two chambers or houses, which were called into existence in most parts of Europe during the last century. The procedure also of continental parliaments is largely modelled on, and copied directly or indirectly from, the procedure of the House of Commons at Westminster. The National Assembly, which was the first product of the French Revolution of 1789, had no rules of procedure, and was a disorderly body. Mirabeau obtained from Dumont, whose name was afterwards so closely associated with Bentham, a digest, which Romilly had made and Dumont had translated into French, of the rules of procedure observed in the British House of Commons. Mirabeau laid a printed copy of this translation on the table of the French Assembly, as a model which might be advantageously followed. But the Assembly would have none of it. 'We are not English,' they said, 'and we don't want anything English'; so it was laid aside. But it did not perish; according to Guizot, it was the basis of the rules of procedure adopted by the French chamber of deputies after the restoration of Louis XVIII. In any case, the procedure then adopted in France was evidently fashioned on an English model, and has influenced the procedure of all other European countries with parliamentary institutions. Thus the rules of parliamentary procedure in all these countries can be traced, directly or indirectly, back to Westminster as their fountain head.

A hundred years after Napoleon's imprisonment at St. Helena another conflagration was blazing in Europe; this time France and Britain were fighting on the same side. When the war which began in 1914 was over, the British system of parliamentary democracy emerged unscathed and there were signs that nations in many parts of the world were ready to pay it the compliment of imitation. By the end of the even fiercer struggle which broke out in 1939, few of those recent experiments had survived. Again, however, the parliament at Westminster was found still to be performing its historic function. It had never ceased to assert its control over the executive; the most powerful minister had scrupulously respected its authority.

The return of peace brought an early resumption of the constitutional process (annually suspended for five war-time years by statutes passed with common consent) of electing a new parliament. The sequel showed no lack of faith in representative institutions. The word 'democracy', as Mr. Attlee reminded the Trade Union Congress when the results of that election were known, means different things in different countries. With us

'democracy is not just majority rule, but majority rule with due respect to the rights of minorities. It means that, while the will of the majority must prevail, there shall be a full opportunity for all points of view to find expression.'

The Master of Balliol affirmed a like belief when addressing the House of Lords in the following year. 'We mean by democracy', he said, 'the kind of thing in which there is a responsible and tolerated opposition.' Those words are the key to the procedure of the parliament at Westminster. If they should cease to be true, there would be an end of government by discussion and government by consent.

GLOSSARY

ADJOURNMENT, MOTION FOR THE.—A step to terminate proceedings, sometimes used to initiate a general discussion or (see p. 118) for a half-hour debate on some current matter of grievance or criticism of the administration.

A motion for the adjournment 'for the purpose of discussing a definite matter of urgent public importance' (under Standing Order No. 8) requires the support of at least 40 members; the occasion must be something more than a personal grievance and must comply with other requirements if the Speaker is to allow it to proceed.

ARMY [AND AIR FORCE] (ANNUAL) BILL.—By the Bill of Rights (1688) the raising and keeping of a standing army within this Kingdom in time of peace without consent of Parliament is declared contrary to law. The annual Bill legalizes the position. Its enactment is one of the reasons why parliament must sit annually.

BLUE BOOKS.—Reports of departments, committees, &c., presented to parliament, with a blue cover.

BUDGET RESOLUTIONS.—The Chancellor of the Exchequer having 'opened his budget' (i.e. surveyed the nation's income and expenditure and outlined his proposals for changes in taxation) the requirements of the revenue make it necessary to pass forthwith the resolutions which embody those changes. They are eventually caught up in the Finance Bill (see p. 92).

CASTING VOTE.—In the Lords if the votes are equal, the decision is recorded in the negative (see p. 177 above). In the Commons the Speaker has a casting vote; usually, where practicable, his principle of impartiality causes him to vote in such manner as not to make the decision of the House final.

CATCHING THE SPEAKER'S EYE.—In the House of Commons when two or more members rise to speak, the Speaker calls on the member whom he first observes. The Chair is often aware of the members who desire to be called on. For the House of Lords procedure see p. 177.

CITATION OF STATUTES.—All Bills coming before Parliament must have a short title. They contain some such clause as 'This Act may be cited as the Housing Act 1930'. Another more complicated and less descriptive method of citation is by regnal year and sessional chapter. Thus the Housing Act 1930 may be cited as '20 & 21 Geo. 5, c. 39', i.e. the 39th Act in the parliamentary session which ran during the 20th and 21st years of King George's reign, reckoned from the date of his accession (6 May 1910).

CLOSURE.—Method of preventing further continuation of debate by obtaining a majority on the motion 'that the question be now put'. At least 100 members must vote in the majority in support of the motion. See also *Guillotine* and *Kangaroo.*

COMMAND PAPERS.—Official publications presented to Parliament by command of His Majesty (at the instance, of course, of a minister). These documents are numbered in the following series:

C. 1 to C. 9550 . .	1870–1899
Cd. 1 to Cd. 9239 . .	1900–1918
Cmd. 1 to —— . .	1919–

COUNT.—On notice being taken that a quorum (see *Quorum*) is not present in the House, members are summoned as for a division (see *Division*). If no quorum be present within two minutes, the House is adjourned. Thus a Bill, or a speaker, is said to be 'counted out'.

COURT OF REFEREES (COMMONS).—Members appointed by the Speaker to decide whether petitions against a Private Bill have a *locus standi*, i.e. a right to be heard on their petition. The court sits in a judicial atmosphere and follows former precedents which are collected in volumes of reported decisions. Refusal to admit petitioners to be heard is becoming rare.

DELEGATED LEGISLATION.—Orders in Council or other orders, regulations, rules of court, &c., made by a Government department or other public body under authority devolved upon it by a statute. Officially published under the name of Statutory Instruments (formerly called Statutory Rules and Orders).

DISSOLUTION.—End of a parliament (not merely of a session) by royal proclamation. It wipes the slate clean of all uncompleted Bills or other proceedings.

DIVISION.—On a division being called in the House of Commons, members outside the Chamber are summoned by bells which ring in the passages, library, smoking-room, &c. The 'Ayes' are directed into the right lobby, the 'Noes' into the left. Tellers are appointed for each party. Officials of the House mark on a list of members' names the members who go past them in each lobby. The tellers report the numbers and the Chair declares the result. See also *Lobby*.

ERSKINE MAY.—Sir Thomas Erskine May (1815–86), first Lord Farnborough, successively assistant librarian of the House of Commons, examiner of Private Bills and taxing-master, and Clerk of the House. Famous for his volume on *Parliamentary Practice* (the standard work now in its 14th edition) and for his *Constitutional History*.

ESTIMATES.—Sessional estimates, showing the grants required in the current year for the navy, army, air force, and civil services, are annually presented to the House of Commons (see pp. 83–5). If more is required, additional or 'supplementary' estimates are laid.

EXEMPTED BUSINESS.—Various matters, specified in Standing Orders, which may be entered upon after the normal time for adjourning the House at the end of the day. Prayers for the annulment of delegated legislation are exempted business.

EXPIRING LAWS.—Various temporary enactments are prolonged by an annual Expiring Laws Continuance Act (see p. 40, for instance, as to the Ballot Act). Periodically the list is reviewed and some of the enactments are made permanent.

GUILLOTINE.—A method of limiting discussion on a Bill by fixing times for voting on its different parts (see p. 120). See also *Kangaroo.*

HYBRID BILL.—A Public Bill which, because it affects private rights, is referred to the Examiners (see p. 67) to ascertain if the Private Business Standing Orders (as to notice to parties affected, &c.) have been complied with.

IRRELEVANCE OR REPETITION IN DEBATE.—Members offending in this respect may, by Standing Order, be directed to discontinue their speech.

JOINT COMMITTEE.—Consists of members of both Houses in equal numbers. A peer usually presides.

KANGAROO.—The power of the Chairman of Ways and Means or Deputy Chairman to select amendments in committee, jumping over some and alighting upon others. The 'Kangaroo closure', drastic and seldom used, limits discussion on a Bill by putting the question on a whole clause or part of a clause irrespective of any amendments. See also *Guillotine*.

KING'S CONSENT (not to be confused with the Royal Assent to Bills, for which see p. 213).—Required on certain Bills where the royal prerogative or other Crown rights are affected. Usually given at the Third Reading stage. Signified to the House by a Privy Councillor.

KING'S RECOMMENDATION.—Owing to the constitutional principle that the Crown (i.e. the Sovereign's responsible advisers who form the Government) alone originates financial business, the king's recommendation is required for proposals of public expenditure. It is signified at the appropriate stage by a Minister of the Crown.

KING'S SPEECH.—At the opening of a Parliament or of a session the 'speech from the Throne' is delivered by the Sovereign in person or, in his absence, by the Lord Chancellor. The Commons are summoned by Black Rod to hear it at the bar of the House of Lords. It contains a statement on foreign affairs and policy and home affairs and policy, and on the proposed programme of legislation. It is followed by the moving of an address of thanks to His Majesty for his gracious speech, by a general debate on the government policy thus announced, and by discussion on amendments usually drawing attention to omissions.

At the close of a session another King's Speech reviews its legislative results.

LAW OFFICERS OF THE CROWN.—For England the Attorney General and Solicitor General; for Scotland the Lord Advocate (whose position and dignity are higher than those of the English Law Officers) and

Solicitor General. Their opinions, given to Government departments, are usually deemed confidential.

LEGISLATION BY REFERENCE.—Strictly the practice of applying the laws about one subject to another subject not quite similar, e.g. extending the Diseases of Animals Acts 'with the necessary modifications and adaptations' to the diseases of poultry, of fish, or of bees. Undesirable because of the uncertainty resulting when the ready-made clothes do not fit.

Less properly the practice of amending an enactment by specific reference to that enactment, thus involving recourse to some other document.

LOBBY—Places near the Chamber where members are to be seen: frequented by journalists with right of access for the purpose of obtaining parliamentary intelligence or gossip ('lobby correspondents') or by other persons seeking to influence members' views (the practice of 'lobbying'). Division lobbies (see *Division*) are corridors through which members pass to record their votes and to which strangers have no access.

MAIDEN SPEECH.—A member's first speech in Parliament. By custom it is free from interruption and it receives compliments from the following speaker.

MAY.—See *Erskine May*

MOVING FOR PAPERS.—A peer may 'call attention' to some subject in the House of Lords and thus initiate a debate; if he also 'moves for papers', he obtains (as mover) a right of reply. After debate and a reply from the Government side the mover usually asks leave to withdraw the motion. There are often no papers to lay.

MOVING FOR WRIT.—When a seat in the House of Commons becomes vacant, the Chief Whip of the party to which the former member belonged moves that the Speaker issue his warrant to the Clerk of the

Crown to make out a new writ to be transmitted to the constituency for a new election.

MOVING THE SPEAKER OUT OF THE CHAIR.—The motion 'That Mr. Speaker do now leave the Chair' gives an opportunity for a debate in the House of Commons, as a preliminary to first going into Committee of Supply (see p. 84) on the navy, army, air, or civil estimates. Amendments may be moved.

The motion asserts the ancient principle that redress of grievances precedes grant of supply.

NAMING A MEMBER.—A member guilty of grossly disorderly conduct may be directed to withdraw for the remainder of the sitting. If he refuses or is otherwise guilty of persistent disregard of the authority of the Chair, the Speaker may 'name' him, whereupon the leader of the House moves that he be suspended from the service of the House.

ORDERS OF THE DAY.—The matters (Bills, &c.) which the House of Commons has ordered to be taken into consideration on the particular day. As soon as question-time is over, the cry 'Orders of the Day' is heard in the lobbies, if there has been no intermediate business.

OUTLAWRIES BILL.—After the King's Speech at the beginning of a new parliament or of a session, both Houses assert their independent right of deliberating without reference to the immediate cause of summons. For this purpose the Commons traditionally give a first reading to a 'Bill for the more effectual preventing of Clandestine Outlawries' (although outlawry has been formally abolished by statute); the Lords give a first reading to a Select Vestries Bill.

PAIRING.—The agreement between two members on opposite sides to abstain from voting (either in a particular division or for a period), thus equalizing the effect of their absence.

PARLIAMENTARY AGENTS.—Legal practitioners who act for the promoters or opponents of Private Bills. Their names must be entered on an official register.

PARLIAMENTARY BAR.—Barristers who practise before committees on opposed Private Bills.

PARLIAMENTARY COUNSEL.—Whole-time official draftsmen of Government Bills and amendments.

PRAYER.—The moving of an address to His Majesty—most commonly an address for the annulment of some Order in Council or set of regulations which has been laid before the House, or for the confirmation of similar documents which have been laid in draft form.

PREAMBLE.—Recitals (of policy or of facts) at the beginning of a Bill or Act. Nowadays rare in Public Bills except where constitutional matters are involved—e.g. in the Government of India Act 1919, or the Statute of Westminster 1931. In Private Bills the preamble explains the promoter's reasons and objects; a Private Bill Committee finds the 'preamble proved' or 'not proved'.

PRIVATE BILL (distinguished from Public Bill).—A Bill for the particular interest or benefit of any person or persons. It begins by petition on the part of the promoters. Its procedure is regulated by a special series of 'Private Business Standing Orders'. See p. 68.

PRIVATE MEMBER'S BILL.—A Public Bill which is not a Government Bill (see p. 59). Occasionally the Government adopt, or arrange facilities for, a Private Member's Bill.

PRIVILEGE.—When, at a new Parliament, the Speaker

attends in the Lords for the royal approval of his election, he claims 'the ancient and undoubted rights and privileges of the Commons'. These include freedom from arrest (now a negligible matter because there is no immunity from imprisonment on a charge for an indictable offence, and imprisonment for debt has long been abolished), freedom of speech, access to the royal person, and the placing of a favourable construction upon the proceedings of the House. Apart from these matters the House deals with many matters as matters of privilege and, in particular, punishes (as breach of privilege) any disrespect to the House on the part of a member or non-member, any disrespect to a member by a non-member (or even, apparently, to a non-member by a member), and any disobedience to the orders of the House or any interference with its procedure.

PROROGATION.—End of a session (not of a parliament). Like a Dissolution, it kills all Bills which have not yet passed; but see p. 68 for the carrying over of Private Bills.

QUORUM.—Minimum number of members required to be present in the House if proceedings are to begin or continue (40 in Commons, 3 in Lords). See also *Count*.

READING OF SPEECHES.—Not permitted, but a speaker may use notes to refresh his memory.

ROYAL ASSENT.—Given to Bills which have been passed by both Houses. The Sovereign seldom gives it in person; he usually appoints a commission to do it on his behalf (see p. 58). See also pp. 191 (Parliament Act procedure) and 74 (Church Assembly Measures).

The President of the United States not infrequently imposes his veto on a Bill passed by Congress. The

Sovereign in Britain could hardly refuse assent since he acts under his Ministers' advice, and they could find other means to stop the progress of a Bill to which they objected. The last refusal was by Queen Anne in 1707.

SELECTION OF AMENDMENTS.—See *Kangaroo.*

SHORT TITLE.—See *Citation of Statutes.*

SPEECH FROM THE THRONE.—See *King's Speech.*

STANDING ORDERS.—Both Houses have permanent rules for their proceedings for Public Business and for Private Business. The rules can be suspended as desired. They do not constitute complete codes because they do not embody all the matters of ancient custom and precedent or rulings by the Chair.

STATUTORY INSTRUMENTS.—The name given by the Statutory Instruments Act 1946 to delegated legislation (see *Delegated Legislation*). The former name, given by the Rules Publication Act 1893 (repealed by the 1946 Act) was Statutory Rules and Orders.

TEN MINUTES RULE.—A simple procedure for a Private Member (when the Government is not monopolizing the whole time of the House) to introduce a Bill, with a time-limit for speeches.

TREASURY BENCH.—The front row of the benches on the Speaker's right hand, occupied by members of the Government.

USUAL CHANNELS.—The party whips, who communicate to one another the wishes and intentions of the Government and the Opposition to facilitate the programme of business.

VOTE OF CENSURE.—A motion by the Opposition attacking the policy of the Government, usually moved by the Leader of the Opposition.

VOTES AND PROCEEDINGS.—The official summary of what

happened in the House of Commons on the previous day.

WHITE PAPERS.—Official returns ordered by the House to be printed; memoranda and statements of policy, &c., prepared for the information of parliament.

BIBLIOGRAPHY

This is a selected list of books which the student will find useful. They will put him on the track of other authorities and sources of information.

I. ORIGIN AND DEVELOPMENT OF THE CONSTITUTION

(*a*) *Documentary Sources*

LODGE, ELEANOR C., and THORNTON, GLADYS A. *English Constitutional Documents (1307–1485)*, 1935

TANNER, J. R. *Tudor Constitutional Documents (1485–1603)*, 1922

Constitutional Documents of the Reign of James I, (1603–1625), 1930

STUBBS, W. *Select Charters and other illustrations of English Constitutional History, from the earliest times to the reign of Edward the First*, 1870

PROTHERO, G. W. *Select Statutes and other Constitutional Documents illustrative of the reigns of Elizabeth and James I*, 1894

(*b*) *Historical Works*

STUBBS, W. *Constitutional History of England*, 1874–8

The fullest and most authoritative history of the English constitution from the earliest times to the beginning of the Tudor dynasty.

HALLAM, H. *Constitutional History of England*, 1827

Covers the period from the accession of Henry VII to the death of George II (1760), and is still of great value for that period.

ERSKINE MAY, SIR T. *Constitutional History of England*

Covers the period from 1760 to 1860, and contains a supplementary chapter dealing with the subsequent ten years. A new edition (1912) contains a very useful third volume by Francis Holland, bringing the history down to the end of 1911.

MAITLAND, F. W. *Constitutional History of England*, 1908

Describes the state of public law at five selected periods: 1307, 1509, 1625, 1702, 1888. The most brilliant and suggestive account that has yet been written of the development of English constitutional history.

TODD, ALPHEUS. *Parliamentary Government in England.* 2nd edition, by his son, 1887–9

A useful book, but out of print and difficult to obtain. A new edition, abridged and revised by the late Sir Spencer Walpole, was published in 1892, and will be found of great value.

PORRITT, E. *The Unreformed House of Commons:* Vol. I, *England and Wales.* Vol. II, *Scotland and Ireland*, 1903

The best description of parliamentary representation before 1832, freely drawn upon in these pages.

PIKE, L. O. *Constitutional History of the House of Lords from original sources*, 1894

Perhaps the best book on this particular subject.

POLLARD, A. F. *The Evolution of Parliament*, 1920. Revised edition, 1926

KEIR, D. L. *Constitutional History of Modern Britain (1485–1937)*, 1938

PASQUET, D. (translated by LAFFAN). *Origin of the House of Commons*, 1925

II. *THE WORKING OF THE CONSTITUTION*

BAGEHOT, W. *The English Constitution*

This little book, which has become a classic, first appeared in the form of articles in the *Fortnightly Review*, was then published in 1867, and describes the English Constitution as it stood in the years 1865 and 1866. To the second edition, published in 1872, was prefixed an introduction describing the changes which had taken place since the passing of the Representation of the People Act of 1867. The book contains the best description extant of Parliament in the Palmerstonian period. It criticizes the theory of the constitution as expounded by Blackstone and De Lolme, and shows that this did not correspond with actual facts. It explains the actual working of what has since been known as the Cabinet system of government, a term to which Bagehot first gave currency.

LASKI, H J. *Parliamentary Government in England*, 1938

JENNINGS, W. IVOR. *Cabinet Government*, 1936
Parliament, 1939

KEITH, A. B. *The Cabinet System (1830–1938)*, 1939

ROSS, J. S. F. *Parliamentary Representation*, 1943

An interesting analysis of the background, age, education, &c., of candidates and members of parliament.

Report from the Select Committee on Offices or Places of Profit under the Crown, 1941

Has a full historical survey of the intricate enactments as to members' disqualification.

III. *THE LAW OF THE CONSTITUTION*

DICEY, A. V. *The Law of the Constitution.* 9th edition, 1939

A well-known work, which has materially influenced

political thought, particularly by the distinction drawn between the law and the conventions of the constitution.

ANSON, SIR W. *The Law and Custom of the Constitution:* Vol. I, *Parliament*, 5th edition (by Sir Maurice Gwyer), 1922. Vol. II (a double volume), *The Crown*, 4th edition (by A. B. Keith), 1935

The standard book on the subject, gives a clear, orderly and full description of the different branches of the government and the way in which they work, with brief sketches of their historical development.

WADE, E. C. S. and PHILLIPS, G. G. *Constitutional Law.* 2nd edition, 1935

JENNINGS, W. I., and YOUNG, C. M. *Constitutional Laws of the British Empire*, 1938.

Selected cases from the courts.

IV. PRACTICE AND PROCEDURE OF PARLIAMENT

ERSKINE MAY, SIR T. *Parliamentary Practice.* 14th edition (by Sir Gilbert Campion), 1946

The most authoritative book on the subject. It is intended for practical use, and is sometimes difficult reading for a student who is not familiar with parliamentary ways and expressions.

REDLICH, JOSEF. *The Procedure of the House of Commons.* Translated from the German by A. E. Steinthal, with an introduction and a supplementary chapter by Sir Courtenay Ilbert. 3 vols., 1908.

Professor Redlich's book is the only historical account of English parliamentary procedure, and is indispensable to the student of that subject. A bibliography is to be found in Vol. II, pp. 10–20.

CAMPION, SIR GILBERT. *Introduction to the Procedure of the House of Commons*, 2nd edition, 1947.

V. THE DRAFTING OF STATUTES

THRING, LORD. *Practical Legislation*, 2nd edition, 1902

The first and simplest statement of the rules of drafting by a great draftsman.

ILBERT, SIR C. P. *Legislative Methods and Forms*, 1901

A standard work, now out of print.

RUSSELL, SIR ALISON. *Legislative Drafting and Forms*, 4th edition, 1938

Specially useful to officials in the British Empire overseas, but contains much useful advice of a general kind.

HERBERT, SIR A. P. *The Ayes have it*, 1937

An entertaining account of the genesis of a Private Member's Bill.

VI. FINANCE

HIGGS, H., C.B. *The Financial System of the United Kingdom*, 1914

By a former Treasury Official of great experience.

YOUNG, E. HILTON (LORD KENNET) and YOUNG, N. A. *The System of National Finance*. 3rd edition, 1936

A very good popular account.

Eleventh Report from the Select Committee on National Expenditure (session 1943–4), 1944

Contains a valuable historical retrospect.

VII. SHORTER AND MORE POPULAR STUDIES

GRAHAM, HARRY. *The Mother of Parliaments*, 1910

A pleasant book for the general public.

GORDON, S. *Your Parliament*, 1945

An accurate, comprehensive, and thoroughly readable exposition by an official of the House of Commons.

BROWN, W. J., M.P. *Everybody's Guide to Parliament*, 1945

A lively account by an active M.P.

FELL, SIR BRYAN. *The Houses of Parliament. A Short Guide to the Palace of Westminster.* Revised edition, by K. R. Mackenzie, 1947.

An admirable little guide-book, dealing with the building, its history, and the daily routine of parliament.

VIII. DOMINION AND OVERSEA CONSTITUTIONS

TODD, A. *Parliamentary Government in the British Colonies*, 1880

Very useful for the period which it covers.

KEITH, A. B. *Responsible Government in the Dominions.* 2 vols. Clarendon Press, 1928

This is an expansion of a little book published in 1909, and is a complete and authoritative work on the subject with which it deals.

KEITH, A. B. *Imperial Unity and the Dominions.* Clarendon Press, 1916

Discusses some of the problems of Imperial Federation.

LOWELL, A. LAWRENCE. *Government and Parties in Continental Europe.* New edition, 1912

For English readers probably the best introduction to the study of the working of parliamentary government on the continent of Europe.

SEIGNOBOS, C. *A Political History of Contemporary Europe since 1814.* Translated from the French, 1904

Shows how European constitutions have grown up and been developed.

BRYCE, VISCOUNT. *The American Commonwealth.* New edition, 1911.

The classical work on the United States. Interesting studies of the constitutions of the United States, of South Africa, and of Australia are to be found in Vol. I of Lord Bryce's *Studies in History and Jurisprudence.* 1901.

WILSON, WOODROW. *Congressional Government,* 1885

Has passed through many editions, and is a very illuminating study.

TEMPERLEY, H. W. V. *Senates and Upper Chambers,* 1910

Contains useful information about the constitution and powers of the legislatures in different countries.

DODD, W. F. *Modern Constitutions,* 1909

A useful American compilation.

QUICK, JOHN, and GARRAN, ROBERT. *Annotated Constitution of the Australian Commonwealth,* 1901

EGERTON, H. E., and GRANT, W. L. *Canadian Constitutional Development,* 1907

KENNEDY, W. P. *The Constitution of Canada, 1534–1937.* 2nd edition, 1938

KENNEDY, W. P. M., and SCHLOSBERG, H. J. *The Law and Custom of the South African Constitution,* 1935

BROGAN, D. W. *The American Political System,* 1933

An admirable statement.

Constitutions of All Countries: Vol. I, *The British Empire,* 1938

The authoritative text, published by H.M. Stationery Office.

INDEX

Abbots, 5, 169
Act of Parliament (see also *Bill*):
  citation, 206
  enactment formula, 12, 14, 61
  enrolment, 154
  Local Act, 63, 66, 70
  short title, 206
Adjournment:
  arrangements, 110–11
  debate on, 97, 100–2, 113, 118
  motion for, 102, 205
  time, 112–13
Air raids, 20, 107–9, 112
Anne, 49, 58, 214
Appropriation accounts, 87–89
Appropriation Acts, 51, 83, 87, 93, 102
Asquith, Herbert Henry, 1st Earl of Oxford and Asquith, 189
Astor, Lady, 48
Attlee, Rt. Hon. C. R., 203

Bagehot, Walter, 30, 38, 130, 218
Ballot Act, 40
Bank of England, 78
Barons, 5–7, 169
Barry, Sir Charles, 106
Bentham, Jeremy, 33, 114, 202
Bill (see also *Act of Parliament: Commons: Legislation*):
  amendments, 63, 183, 208
Bill (*contd.*):
  closure, 119, 120, 206
  committee stage, 54–7, 65
  drafting, 13–14, 59, 61, 212, 220
  Finance Bills, 56, 179, 181, 189
  genesis and procedure, 61–66
  Government Bills, 53, 60, 199
  hybrid, 208
  introduction, 53, 58–9, 62, 115, 177
  Local Bills, 66, 148
  Lords' amendments, 57, 184–5, 192
  money, 12, 179, 181, 190–1
  petition for, 9, 13, 68
  preamble, 67, 212
  Private Bills, 66–70, 126, 148, 200, 212
  private member's, 37, 53, 59, 60, 118, 199, 212
  provisional order confirmation, 69
  report stage, 57, 64, 66, 122
  royal assent, 11, 57–8, 74, 127, 190–2
  royal veto (obsolete), 14, 58, 213–4
  Scottish, 54
  selection of amendments, 183, 208
  sent to Lords, 57
  ten minutes' rule, 214
  three readings, 17, 53–8
  time table, 120, 122–3, 136

Bishops, 5, 170
Black Rod. See *Lords*
Broadcasting, 152, 166
Bryce, James, 1st Viscount, 186, 202, 222
Budget, 90–2, 94, 205
Burgage, 26–7
Burke, Edmund, 32, 94, 135, 139

Cabinet system, 19, 62, 128–33, 194, 197
Casting vote, 177, 205
Censure, vote of, 100, 182
Chancellor of the Exchequer, 90, 94
Chartism, 36
Chiltern hundreds, 50
Church Assembly, 74, 109
Churchill, Rt. Hon. Winston Spencer, 107–8
Civil list, 79
Clergy, 5–7, 11, 48
Clerk of the Crown, 50, 58
Clerk of the Parliaments, 58, 127
Closure, 119, 120, 206
Cobbett, William, 164
Coke, Sir Edward, 113
Command papers, 98, 206
Committees:
- Commons, 54, 121–2, 128
- constitution, 98–9
- Ecclesiastical, 74
- Elizabethan origin, 17
- Estimates, 88–9
- joint, 56
- Kitchen, 128
- National Expenditure, 88–90
- of Selection, 54, 128
- Private Bills, 67–8
- Public Accounts, 87–8
- Publications and Debates, 128

Committees (*contd.*):
- select, 56, 89
- sittings, 128
- Special Orders (Lords), 74
- standing, 54–6, 119, 121–2
- Statutory Rules and Orders, 73
- Supply, 84-7, 101
- Ways and Means, 84, 90, 92
- whole House, 18, 55–6, 84, 126, 128

Commons (see also *Committees: Elections: Parliament*):
- adjournment debates, 97, 113, 118, 205
- clerk, 126, 154, 189
- conferences with Lords, 186–8
- court of referees, 207
- divisions, 120–1, 137, 207, 210
- exempted business, 113, 208
- financial functions, 76, 82, 93, 178, 181, 189–91
- hours of sitting, 111–12
- impeachments, 174
- Journals, 153
- members:
  - benevolent fund, 51
  - correspondence, 148
  - disqualification, 48
  - duties, 139
  - naming, 117
  - numbers, 34, 43, 46–7, 107
  - oath, 47
  - office of profit, 49
  - pairing, 211
  - payment, 23, 50–1, 141–143
  - privilege, 212–13
  - retirement, 50

Commons (*contd.*):
officials, 126
order, 115, 117
orders of the day, 113, 211
place of sitting, 16, 20, 105, 109, 154
prayers, 112
privileges, 114, 180–2, 191
question-time, 74, 96–8, 113
reports of debates, 159
strangers in, 166–8
taxation, 11, 90, 181, 189–91
using Lords' chamber, 109, 112, 167
votes and proceedings, 157, 214
Comptroller and Auditor General, 82, 87
Conferences (between the two Houses), 187–8
Consolidated fund, 78–9
Consolidated Fund Acts, 86, 93, 102
Cornish boroughs, 24–5, 31, 34
Cromwell, Oliver, 18, 153

Defence of the Realm Acts, 71
Delegated legislation:
control by—
courts of law, 72
Parliament, 72, 113
grandchildren of statutes, 71
negative and affirmative procedure, 72
prayers against, 72, 208, 212
scrutinizing committee, 73
separation of powers, 194–195
Special Orders Committee, 74

Delegated legislation (*contd.*):
statuory instruments, 70, 214
Statutory Rules and Orders, 70, 207, 214
war-time use, 71, 122
d'Ewes, Sir Symonds, 17, 115
Disraeli, Benjamin, Earl of Beaconsfield, 39, 134
Dodington, Bubb, 25

Elections:
absent voters, 44
alternative vote, 45
ballot, 40
blind voters, 40
borough franchise, 23
candidate's—
deposit, 44
expenses, 44, 145
county franchise, 22
disputed election, 50
faggot voters, 23
pocket boroughs, 24
postal voting, 47
proportional representation, 45
proxy voting, 44, 47
register of electors, 34–5, 44
return, evidence of, 50
women voters, 43, 46
writ, moving for, 210
Elizabeth, 15–17, 24, 155
Emergency Powers (Defence) Acts, 71
Estates, Three, 6, 11
Estimates, 83, 85, 88–9, 101, 208
Examiners, 67, 208

Finance (see also *Estimates: Taxation*):
annual Act, 92
Bill rejected by Lords, 92, 181, 189

Finance (*contd.*) :
  borrowing, 93
  budget, 90–2, 205
  Commons' powers, 76–7, 83–84, 178, 189–91
  Crown and parliament, 11, 76–7, 85, 92
  King's recommendation, 77, 209
  national debt, 79
  Parliament Act effect, 190–191
  permanent charges, 79
  supply days, 85–6, 101
  ways and means, 84
Fox, Charles James, 27
Franchise. See *Elections*
France, 1, 6, 19, 32, 94, 97

George III, 130
Gladstone William Ewart, 30, 40, 92, 181
Grievances, redress of, 8, 85, 101, 154, 211
Guillotine, 120, 208

Hansard, 97, 152, 164–5
Herbert, Sir Alan, 59

Ilbert, Sir Courtenay, vi
Impeachment, 174, 194–5
Ireland:
  consolidated fund, 78
  Eire, 46
  Irish peers, 48, 171–2
  Government of Ireland Act (1914), 192
  Northern Ireland, 46, 48, 101–2, 123
  reform Act, 35
  union with, 34, 171

Jefferson, Thomas, 198
Johnson, Samuel, 161–2
Joint committees, 56, 208
Journals, 16, 153
Judges, 49 ,80, 111, 126, 173

Kangaroo, 208
King:
  and Commons, 14, 17
  and Speaker, 124
  influence of, 130
  King's consent, 209
  King's council, 7, 8, 10
  King's recommendation, 77, 209
  King's speech, 8, 100, 109, 197, 209
  opening parliament, 111
  proclamations, 110
  royal assent to Bills (&c.), 57–8, 74, 190–1, 213
Knights of the shire, 5–7, 41

Law officers, 122, 209
Legislation (see also *Act of Parliament: Bill: Delegated legislation*):
  'crisis' law-making, 71
  general procedure, 52
  Government Bills and time, 37–8, 53, 59–61
  Measures of Church Assembly, 74
  official draftsmen, 61, 212
  provisional orders, 69
  referential, 210
  special procedure orders, 70
  speeding up, 122
Lords (see also *Parliament*):
  amending Commons Bills, 57, 184–5, 188, 192
  business, 176
  early history, 169–71
  Commons privileges, 180–181
  conferences with Commons, 186–8

Lords (*contd.*) :
finance powers restricted, 76–7, 92, 178, 182, 189–91
impeachments, 175
Journals, 153
judges summoned, 8
judicial appeals, 173, 175
life peers, 173–4
Lord Chairman of Committees, 127
Lord Chancellor, 127, 173, 176–7
lords of appeal in ordinary, 173
membership, 169
moving for papers, 210
officials, 127
Parliament Act, 1911, 57, 190–1
place of sitting, 106, 109
prayers, 175–6
procedure, 57, 176
proposals for reform, 186
rejection of Finance Bill, 181, 189
revising body, 183
Special Orders Committee, 74
Standing Orders, 176
Lowther, James William, Viscount Ullswater, Speaker of the House of Commons, 43

Macaulay, Lord, 188
Maiden speech, 210
Maitland, F. W., 2, 21, 217
Matrimonial Causes Act, 1937, 59
May, Erskine, 18, 76, 173, 207
Ministerial responsibility, 73–4, 88, 129, 131–3, 197
Ministers of the Crown Act, 1937, 51, 134
Minority views, 103, 203–4
Model Parliament, 1, 5
Money Bill. See *Bill*
Montesquieu, 195
Montfort, Simon de, 5

National debt, 79–82

Oath of member, 47–8, 51
Obstruction, 116
Office of profit, 48–9, 129
Opposition, 51, 101, 134, 136
Orders. See *Delegated legislation* ; *Standing Orders*
Outlawries Bill, 211

Palace of Westminster, 20, 104
Palgrave, Sir Reginald, 18
Palmerston, Lord, 38, 171
Parliament (see also *Commons: Lords*) :
adjournments, 110
dissolution, 110, 207
duration, 19, 46, 110, 189, 191–2
history, 1
hours, 111, 176
judge in, 8, 49
law and custom of, 113–14, 214
legislation. See *Act of Parliament*: *Bill*
opening, 11, 111
prorogation, 68, 110, 213
quorum, 213
session, 16, 57–8, 110, 213
summoning, 110
Parliament Act, 1911, 19, 57, 77, 190–2
Parliamentary agents, 69, 212
Parliamentary bar, 69, 212

Parliamentary counsel, 61, 212
Parliamentary papers, 158
Party system, 74, 102, 107, 133–4, 143–5
Peel, Arthur Wellesley, 1st Viscount, Speaker of the House of Commons, 114
Peers (see also *Lords*):
  creation, &c., 170–1
  life peers, 173
  privilege, 175
  Scottish and Irish, 48, 171–2
Petitions, 9, 10, 13, 68, 113
Pitt, William, 19, 78, 111
Porritt, Edward, 24, 125
Prayer-book Measure, 75
Press, 152, 166–8
Prime Minister, 51, 131–3
Private Bills. See *Bill*
Private members:
  adjournment debate, 100–1, 113, 118, 205
  Bills of, 59–61
  motions, 100
  party duties, 137
  questions, 96–8
Privilege, 113–14, 180–1, 212–13
Prorogation, 68, 110, 213
Provisional orders, 69

Questions to ministers, 96–8, 113
Quorum, 213

Redistribution of seats, 41–2, 47
Reform Bill, 20, 24, 33–6, 38, 189
Representation of the People Acts, 39–46
Royal assent. See *Bill*

Saladin tithe, 4
Scotland:
  Bills affecting, 54
  peerages, 48, 171–2
  reform Act, 35
  union with, 34, 171, 186
Septennial Act, 19, 191
Serjeant-at-Arms, 112, 117, 127
Session 16, 57–8, 110, 213
Sheriff, 5, 22–4
Sinking fund, 80
Smith, Sir Thomas, 16
Speaker:
  appointment, 124
  at prayers, 112
  at royal assent, 58
  authority, 125
  casting vote, 205
  claims privileges, 114
  deputy, 126
  impartiality, 125, 201
  King's nominee, 55
  mace, 112, 126
  money Bills, 190–1
  moved out of the chair, 211
  naming a member, 211
  powers, 116–7
  question-time, 97–8
  rulings, 115, 125
  seat, 125
  Speaker's conferences, 43, 45–6
  writ for election, 210
Special orders, 70, 74
Special procedure orders, 70
Spender, J. A., 150, 152
Standing committees. *See* Committees
Standing Orders:
  Commons Private Business, 67–8, 148, 180, 214

Standing Orders (*contd.*) :
Commons Public Business, 54, 112, 114, 116, 118, 214
Lords, 67–8, 176, 214
Statute Law Committee, vii–viii
Statutory Instruments Act, 73, 207, 214
Statutory Rules and Orders, 70, 73, 207, 214
Strafford, Thomas Wentworth, Earl of, 18
Strangers (admission), 127, 166–8
Supply days, 85–6, 101

Taxation (see also *Finance*):
Bills, 92
Commons' functions, 76–7, 83, 93, 178
Crown initiative, 76-7
King's power restricted, 2, 11
representation and, 5
Temple, Sir Richard, 151
Treasury:
bench, 134, 214
draftsmen, 61
estimates, 83
retrenchment, 94
whips, 135
Trevelyan, Sir George, 27, 31, 151

Ullswater, Lord, 43
United States, 193
University franchise, 42–3

Wales, 23, 34, 192
War:
air raid damage, 108–9
expenditure, 88
finance, 83
legislation, 71, 122
postponed elections, 46
procedure, 53, 54, 121
regionalization, 123
secret sessions, 168
sittings, 112
Waste, Statute of, 9
Ways and Means:
chairman, 84, 117, 126
committee, 84, 86–7, 90
Westminster:
Hall, 14, 20, 106
Palace, 20, 104, 106, 109
Whips, 74, 135, 137, 214
White papers, 98, 122, 206
Witenagemot, 2
Women:
in Commons, 48, 172
not in Lords, 170, 172
voters, 43, 46

Printed in Great Britain by Butler & Tanner Ltd., Frome and London

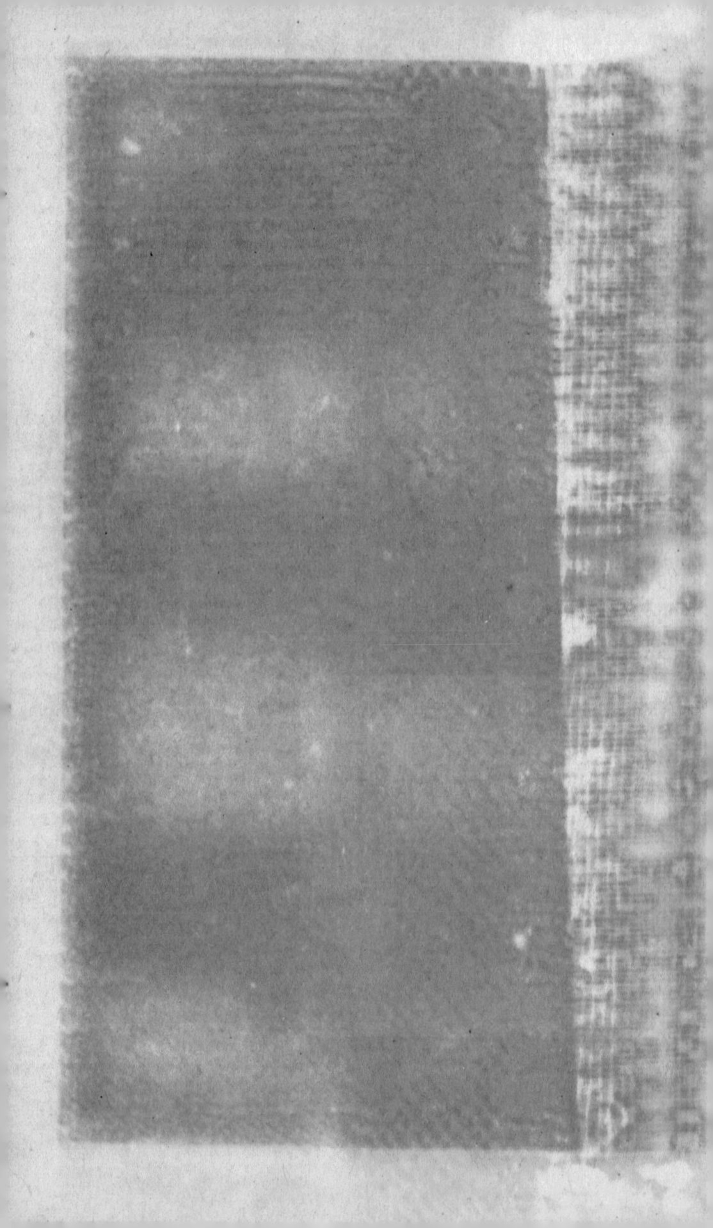